BUDAPEST
ART AND HISTORY

DELIA METH-COHN

FLOW EAST

General Coordinator
Nathalie Shashou

Photographs
Zsolt Szaboky

Design
Carla Sello

Special thanks to
Steven R. Kopits

Museum photographs
Museum of Fine Arts / Dénes Józsa
National Gallery / Levente Szepsy Szücs
National Museum / Károly Szelenyi

Produced by Summerfield Press, Florence
Printed in Italy by Litografica Faenza Group

CONTENTS

9 Introduction

10 Map of the City

13 Buda Castle Hill

39 Pest Inner City

71 Andrássy út and Heroes' Square

93 Riverside Buda

109 Óbuda and Margaret Island

117 Erzsébetváros: the Jewish District

123 Chronology

126 Useful information

Outside Hungary there is no life; if there is, it is not like this.
(Anonymous)

God bless Hungary with prosperity and good fortune, Extend your protective arm when it faces the enemy, Torn by fate since ancient times, Bring to it glad years to come; Its people have suffered enough For the past and the future.
(Ferenc Kölcsey, National Anthem, 1828)

Many people think Hungary once was, I would like to believe it will be!
(Istvan Szechenyi, 1830)

INTRODUCTION

Budapest is the ultimate turn-of-the-century city. Its fascination stems as much from an irresistable urban energy as from centuries of rich historical sediment. Despite the sharp contrast between the twin cities of Buda and Pest, divided by the powerful flow of the Danube and united only in 1872, both radiate the aspirations of the era. In Pest, the proud neo-Classical unity of the buildings, enlivened at intervals by decorative flecks of art nouveau and extravagant eclecticism, obscures the remnants of the city's less glorious medieval and Baroque past. In Buda the pattern is turned on its head. The winding old-world alleyways are lined with colourful Baroque palaces, shallow-domed steam baths built by the Turks during their long occupation of the city dot the bank of the river, and the Royal Palace boasts a long line of royal residents stretching back into the Middle Ages. But the powerful skyline of Buda is more than anything a late 19th century remake, a patriotic fusion of ancient Hungarian motifs with the belief in a glorious national future.

1. Gül Baba tomb
2. Király baths
3. St. Anne's Church
4. Parliament
5. Fisherman's Bastion
6. Mátyás Church
7. Chain Bridge
8. Post Office Savings Bank
9. Opera House
10. Music Academy
11. Heroes' Square
12. Museum of Fine Arts
13. St. Stephen's Basilica
14. Vörösmarty Square
15. Vigadó Concert Hall
16. Royal Palace
17. Inner City Parish Church
18. Dohány Synagogue
19. Citadella
20. Gellért Hotel and Baths
21. Central Market Hall
22. National Museum
23. Museum of Applied Arts

Lehel u.

Újpesti rkp.

Szent István körút

Kossuth
Lajos
tér

Alkotmány u.

Báthory

Nádor

Szabadság
tér

8●

Roosevelt
tér

József Attila u.

Belgrad

14●

15●

Erzsébet
híd

Szent Gellért rakpart

Szabadság

híd

Műegyetem rakpart

Közraktár u.

20●

Lehel
tér

Váci

Teréz

Bajcsy - Zsilinszky út

Podmaniczky u.

Andrássy

Oktogon

9

Király

Deák
F.tér

Károly Krt.

Dob

Király

17● Szabad s. út

Kossuth L. u.

Múzeum Krt.

Vámház krt.

21●

22

Kálvin
tér

Üllői

13

18●

Wesselényi

Rákóczi

Dohány

Baross

23●

út

Dózsa György út

12●

11

Kodály
körönd

Rottenbiller u.

körút

10●

Erzsébet körút

Dob

Wesselényi

körút út

Blaha
L. tér

Népszínház u.

Körút

József

Baross
tér

Mező Imre út

Baross u.

Ferenc körút

Üllői út

1. Budapest History Museum
2. National Gallery
3. Museum of Contemporary History
4. Dísz tér
5. Fisherman's Bastion
6. Mátyás Church
7. Tancsics Mihály utca
8. Magdalene Tower

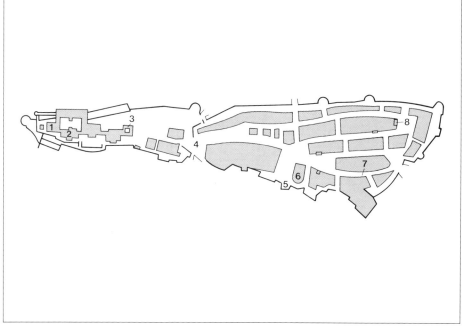

The Chain Bridge at night.

BUDA CASTLE HILL

The **Széchenyi Chain Bridge** (Lánchíd) was the first permanent link between Buda and Pest. Before it was completed in the revolutionary year of 1848, the only connection between the two contrasting cities had been a pontoon bridge. Every morning and evening it was raised to let barges pass down river; every winter it was dismantled to avoid being destroyed by powerful ice floes. But the bridge, with its solid arches and graceful curves looping across the green-grey flow of the Danube, is far more than a physical link. It symbolises Budapest's turbulent emergence as a world city, fired with national pride but striving to become an integral part of Europe; squirming under the fetters of Habsburg rule but fearful of an independent fate surrounded by hostile neighbours.

The bridge was the brain-child of Count István Széchenyi, known as the "Greatest Magyar" for his key role in Hungary's 19th century development. In December 1820, he was stranded for a week in Pest waiting for the Danube to ice over so he could attend his father's funeral in Buda. With this experience in mind, Széchenyi visited England to see the new iron suspension bridges which could solve the technical problems that had made a stone bridge impossible. He returned with two men, William Tierney Clark, who designed the bridge, and Adam Clark who oversaw the construction, fell in love with a Hungarian woman and spent the rest of his life in Budapest. Széchenyi's revolutionary vision went beyond the purely pragmatic. Until then, nobles were exempt from all taxes and tolls; but on this bridge, the Count insisted, everybody would pay the toll. The political implications of this first blow to feudal privileges were clear to everybody. One noble insisted he would make the two-day ride upstream to the next ferry rather than demean himself by paying a toll. The emerging radical leader, Lajos Kossuth, saw it as a first step towards civil equality.

By the time the bridge was finished in 1848, these political conflicts had come to a head. Széchenyi's reformist path to national greatness had given way to Kossuth's vision of a Hungary free from Habsburg rule and aristocratic privilege. Fired by the news of revolutions in Vienna, Milan and Paris, and the inspiring patriotic poetry of Sándor Petöfi, the citizens of Budapest rebelled. At first the ageing Habsburg emperor, Ferdinand V, gave into their demands for self-government. A cabinet was formed under Kossuth, with Széchenyi as reluctant Minister of Transport until severe depression forced him into an insane asylum where he later committed suicide. But once Franz Joseph I took over the Habsburg reigns, the story changed.

Page 6
The view across the Chain Bridge to Pest.

Page 8
The roof of Lechner's art nouveau Museum of Applied Arts.

13

The Austrian army stormed into Buda and Pest, but in 1849 faced a rapidly formed Hungarian army. Holed up in Buda, the Habsburgs threatened to blow up the new Chain Bridge if the army crossed. Dynamite was laid, and the officer in charge, finding no willing candidates, lit the fuse with his cigar. The bridge survived with little damage, but the officer was blown to pieces. With the help of the Russian Czar, Franz Joseph managed to quell the revolution, and the bridge was finally inaugurated on November 21, 1849. Almost a hundred years later, the German army, having lost Pest, blew up all the bridges as it retreated to Buda. The bridge was restored to its old glory and re-inaugurated symbolically on November 21, 1949. Crossing the bridge along its airy walkways, past the friendly lions that guard both arches, Buda looms as a steep wooded hill, topped by the monumental length of the Royal Palace and the spire of the Mátyás Church, and pierced through with the monumental pointed arch of Adam Clark's now exhaust-filled tunnel. At Clark Ádám tér, the Sikló (funicular) splits the hill from top to bottom; although this is the quickest way up to Castle Hill, the winding stone stairways leading up from the right of the tunnel have a dreamy charm and a multiplicity of views that shouldn't be missed. The steps emerge on **Dísz tér**, the main market square in the Middle Ages, with different days for the Hungarians, Germans and Jews who populated Buda at the time. The peaceful streets converge on a discordant blackened ruin of a building, the former **Ministry of Defence**. Pitted with holes and missing its top layer, the building is a jarring but fascinating reminder of how the whole district looked after the Red Army finally forced the Germans to surrender following a month-long battle in 1945 — the thirty-first siege suffered by Buda Castle since its beginning in 1243. Since the end of the 19th century, this had been the government and diplomatic district, but the painstaking post-war renovation took so long that most of the officials moved down to Pest, leaving Castle Hill a peaceful oasis of museums and cultural institutes.

The streets running off Dísz tér are far more beautiful further down, so it's worthwhile resisting the entry into town for a moment. Instead walk past the marvellously strutting statue of a Hussar, created in 1932 by Zsigmond Kisfaludi Stróbl, a master of powerful militaristic sculpture. The **Tóth Árpád setany** runs to the right along the city walls, lined by old houses and chestnut trees. Beyond the tangle of new buildings directly below (around the South (Déli) station), the undulating villa-covered Buda hills rise into the distance. Turn right into the narrow Szentháromság utca, which opens on to the graceful equestrian statue of András Hadik (György Vastagh, 1937), commander of Buda Castle under Empress Maria Theresa. The horse's testicles are said to bring luck and are correspondingly shiny! The street is drawn towards the vertical neo-Gothic lines of the Mátyás church, but be careful not to miss on the left the **Ruszwurm coffee-house** at No. 7. Here the decor and the quality complement each other. The cakes — crème slices, apple pies — are delicious, and the tiny cafe room in its largely original Viennese Biedermeier furnishings (from 1824) is as cozy as an overstuffed living-room. Across from the cafe, the elegant white facade of the

The funicular running up to Castle Hill.

The Baroque Trinity Column intended to ward off the plague.

Right
A side view of the tiled roof and Gothic pinnacles of the Mátyás Church.

former Buda town hall, built in 1692 shortly after the ousting of the Turks, leads into Szentháromság tér (Holy Trinity Square), the focal point of Castle Hill. The voluptuous **Baroque column** in the centre - a familiar site across Catholic Central Europe — was erected in 1713 to ward off further bouts of the plague. Take a closer look at the relief plaque facing the church. Behind the anguished and ailing citizens of Buda, is the castle district as it looked in the 18th century, the Mátyás Church topped with the typical onion-shaped spire of the Baroque era. To the left of the column is the former Ministry of Finance, built in 1906 in an extravagant eclectic style, with a colourful tiled roof and spiky towers that competed for attention with the church. After the war, renovators toned down the partly destroyed building to suit its reduced function as a hostel and cultural center, leaving the eye to focus on the strange proportions and colourful Zsolnay pyrogranite tiles of the **Mátyás Church**.

More than any other building in Budapest, the Mátyás Church (or the Church of Our Lady) has suffered the humiliations and celebrated the rather fewer victories that Hungary has endured during its long history. A church is thought to have been built on this site in 1015 as King István's offering to the German settlers of Castle Hill. This church was destroyed during the first of Hungary's many defeats, the Tatar invasions of 1240-1, but King Béla IV responded to the request of the privileged and growing German community and built a Romanesque church here, dedicated to the Virgin Mary. When the Árpád dynasty died out in 1301, the congregation of the Church of Our Lady refused to recognise the succession of the Vatican-supported Angevin king, Charles Robert. In a wonderful tour de force, they formally excommunicated Pope Boniface VIII along with all his priests and bishops in 1303. Such hubris lasted only a few years, and Charles Robert was crowned here in 1309. His son, Lajos the Great, rebuilt the church in contemporary Gothic style (much as it looks today). In 1444, following a victory against the Turks in the Balkans, King Ulászló Jagello and his commander, János Hunyadi, celebrated a thanksgiving mass for the salvation of Christendom (Ulászló was killed in battle later that year; Hunyadi went on to defeat the Turks at Belgrade in 1456, but died of plague a few weeks later). Hunyadi's son, who became the popular Renaissance King Mátyás Corvinus was crowned here in 1458 at the age of 14, and was married twice in the Church, first to the short-lived Bohemian princess, Catherine of Podebrad, and then to Beatrix, princess of Naples. When the Turks took their revenge and occupied Buda Castle in 1541, the church was turned into a mosque overnight, ready for the Sultan to hold a thanksgiving service to Allah. Over the 145 years of occupation, the walls were whitewashed and painted with inscriptions from the Koran. With Habsburg liberation in 1686, the zealous Jesuits took over and sandwiched the church between a monastery and a seminary, systematically covering over the Gothic stone-work with the curvaceous Baroque facades and dark mystical interior that embodied the counter-reformation throughout the Habsburg lands. After the 1867 Compromise, Emperor Franz Joseph and his astoundingly beautiful wife, Elizabeth, (who had taught herself Hungarian and was

extremely popular in Budapest) were crowned in the church to the music of Franz Liszt's "Coronation Mass". It was the Emperor who requested that the Baroque accretions be removed and the church be restored to its Gothic glory (this was the Ringstrasse era when neo-Gothic and neo-everything-else buildings were being erected in Vienna). The architect Frigyes Schulek set about his task by studying old plans and paintings of the church and, removing the centuries of overlay, discovered the remains of medieval wall-painting, vaulting and statuary. The rest was inspired by the fertile turn-of-the-century imagination. The church was badly damaged during the 1945 siege of Buda, but the restoration was faithful to Schulek's work. The communist era left the church, for once, untouched.

The interior of the church is remarkably intimate. For all its soaring pillars and vaulted ceilings, the usual Gothic sense of elevation is counteracted by the warm colours of the intricate folk designs covering the entire wall space, the work of Bertalan Székely and Károly Lotz. The impression is vaguely oriental or Byzantine, interspersed with swirling art nouveau, a motif that frequently emerges in the architecture of this time in its attempt to define the place of Hungary between East and West. To the left of the entrance is a small Loretto chapel. Behind its black wrought iron gate, whimsically intertwined with a golden rose and leaves, is a red marble statue of the Madonna and Child, donated by King Ulászló II in 1515 in gratitude for narrowly escaping assassination. During the Turkish occupation, the citizens of Buda hid the statue in a wall. As the Habsburg troops launched their final onslaught against the Turks in 1686, a gunpowder store behind the wall exploded and the Madonna sprang out, putting the fear of God into the Turks who surrendered the next day. The legends's veracity is rather dented by the statue's 18th century appearance; maybe she suffered irreparable damage during her divine fall.

On the other side of the steps, above the baptismal font, is an unusual spiral window portraying the lamb of god. The four waterfalls that flow down from the window represent the main rivers of Hungary — the Danube, Drava, Tisza and Sava — immortalized by four silver stripes on the Hungarian coat of arms. Below and to the left, the stone carving of two apostles holding the Bible is from the late 13th century, one of the few genuine relics of the old Gothic church. The triptych painting (by Lotz) shows Pope Calixtus II ruling that church bells all over Christendom be rung daily at noon in recognition of Hunyadi's victory over the Turks in 1456.

The regal leather-bound thrones of the first side chapel make a perfect resting point to scrutinise the St. Imre altar. The four paintings depict the death of King István's only son while out hunting. The event had a gruesome consequence for the Árpád lineage. King István, crowned by the Pope in 1000, refused to allow his younger brother, less taken by Christianity than himself, to succeed him. His remedy was thorough if a little overdone — he arranged to have molten lead poured into his sibling's ear. Paganism was not entirely eliminated by this move. Bishop Gellért (the third statue on the altar after István and Imre), Imre's tutor, was rolled down what is now Gellért hill into the Danube by a group of rebels

Károly Lotz's stained glass window in the Mátyás Church.

loyal to a pagan rival to the throne. All three were sainted in 1083. Those who suggested that the molten lead trick was hardly a qualification for sainthood were told that István's Bavarian wife, Gisela, was behind the evil — a story worthy of Shakespearean treatment! The next chapel houses the sarcophagi of Béla III (1172-1196) and his wife, Anna Chatillon, brought in the 19th century from their original burial ground in the city of Székesfehérvár. Their removal was not least a manoeuvre on the part of Franz Joseph to establish some Hungarian legitimacy in time for his coronation in 1867. Anna Chatillon was related to the Habsburgs by marriage. The plaque on the far side of the grave traces Franz Joseph's royal descent from the Magyar tribal leader, Árpád.

Beyond the altar is the entrance to the **Church Museum** which is well worth visiting not so much for the individual objects but because it gives access to the underground crypts, a tiny chapel, the royal oratory and the gallery. It is here, also, that the coronation of Franz Joseph and Elizabeth is commemorated. Their red satin coronation stools and garments are on display in the royal oratory, along with contemporary depictions of the event. Outside the chapel, Elizabeth's famed beauty is captured in an adoring white marble statue by György Zala; inside, strangely out of place among a collection of jewelled ornaments, is the lace-covered skull of the wife of László Hunyadi, King Mátyás's elder brother, beheaded in the Buda Palace courtyard by the previous king — a Habsburg! From the gallery, there is an excellent view of the stained glass windows, designed by Schulek, Székely and Lotz, and depicting legends from the lives of the Virgin Mary, St. Erzsébet and St. Margit (sister and daughter of Béla IV respectively).

Before leaving the church, notice on the wall by the entrance the endlessly reproduced raven motif. This was the heraldic symbol of King Mátyás (thus his Latin name, Corvinus), inherited from his father János Hunyadi. As a young man, Hunyadi became aware of his crusading mission while dozing in a forest by the sudden appearance of a raven carrying a ring in its mouth. Two of the church spires are topped by copper ravens, Schulek's innovation, intended to cement the semi-official renaming of the church.

To complement the church's new appearance, and as part of the city's beautification campaign on the occasion of the 1896 Millennium Celebration (1000 years since the nomadic Magyar tribes moved from the Volga bend into the Danube basin led by Árpád), Schulek came up with the idea of creating the **Fisherman's Bastion** (Halászbástya), a white neo-Romanesque fantasy of cloistered walkways and pinnacles, commanding a splendid view over the Danube to Pest. In line with the Millennium concept, the seven turrets represent the seven Magyar tribes, bearing such exotic Finno-Ugric names as Ond and Kond. Each of the chiefs has his statue in the complex, and the steps leading down to the Watertown are dotted with figures from János Hunyadi to St. George and the Dragon (a copy of the Prague original). By the South Bastion is the equestrian statue of King and Saint István (Alajos Stróbl, 1906), bearing the double apostolic cross that represents Hungary's conversion to Christianity. The Fisherman's Bastion was certainly

The fairy-tale pinnacles of the Fisherman's Bastion.

21

A Renaissance relief of King Mátyás, now ornamenting the Hilton Hotel.

never a defensive structure, and the origin of its name is a mystery — nearby medieval fish markets and the defensive role of fishermen's guilds are the most popular explanations. Despite the unavoidable sensation of walking into a 'B' movie set, heightened by the ever-present guitar players and colourful peasant vendors, the views are compelling. The Buda Hills to the left are stopped abruptly by an alien settlement of white concrete blocks at Óbuda (ironically the oldest part of the city) which then give way to the romantic rooftops of the Watertown. Across the Danube, intersected by the wooded Margaret Island, are the landmarks of Pest, the red-domed Parliament and the green-domed Basilica, both 96 meters high in patriotic homage to the 896 AD arrival of the Magyar tribes. The bridges span the river into the distance, their names marking the highpoints of recent Hungarian history — Széchenyi Chain Bridge, Elizabeth Bridge, Liberation Bridge (renamed after 1945, previously Franz Joseph Bridge) and Petöfi Bridge (previously named after the inter-war leader, Admiral Horthy). In the smoggy distance lies Csepel Island, the industrial cauldron of Budapest, overlaid from this perspective by Gellért Hill and the Citadella.

The aspect of unreality that so pervades the Fisherman's Bastion is heightened by its proximity to the **Hilton Hotel**, considered by some a masterpiece of conservation, not for its rather ugly (officially neutral!) 1970s facade, but for the way it encompasses the Gothic remains of an old Dominican monastery. These can be seen from the Bastion, but it is best to go back around the Mátyás church to the hotel's main entrance. Between the modern building on the left and what used to be a Baroque Jesuit college on the right, the hotel is dissected by a 13th century stone church tower, decorated with an intricate Renaissance relief of King Mátyás and topped by a peculiar rocket-shaped concrete tower which houses the Hilton Casino! From the lobby bar, the vast windows are filled by the elevating vision of an ancient ruined nave, its broken walls revealing the neo-Gothic spires of the parliament across the river. Steps run down to the old monastery cloisters, interesting despite the dated bottle-bottom decor.

Leaving this ambivalent mixture of architectural and life-styles, the golden yellow harmony of the Fortuna restaurant across the square is a relief. During the brief glow of Renaissance culture under King Mátyás Corvinus (1458-1490), this became in 1473 the **printery** of András Hess, responsible for the beautifully bound and illustrated printed codices, known as Corvinas. In keeping with this tradition, the courtyard houses a wonderful pavilion-style cafe-bookshop called Litea (literature + tea), with numerous tables and chairs where browsers are served with tea or coffee. The bookshop has an excellent collection of English-language books on Hungary.

Táncsics Mihály utca, curving down from the Hilton, is a street of history-filled Baroque palaces. During the strained years of Admiral Horthy's increasingly fascist regime (1919-1944), the palace at No. 1 housed the British Embassy. The building caught fire during the last days of the German occupation of Buda in February 1945, forcing the residents into the cellar. When the Germans finally raised a white flag on the Royal Palace on February 12, the staff hoisted the

Union Jack over the wreck of the building and waited for the arrival some hours later of the Soviet tanks on Dísz tér. The **Museum of Music History** (Zenetörténeti Múzeum) at No. 7 is a pearl of restrained Baroque. Its facade is adorned by the elegant curve of a black wrought iron balcony and its well-proportioned courtyard exudes a melancholy air of more harmonious times. The museum itself is only for historical instrument enthusiasts. Further down at No. 9, the plain two-toned yellow building was, in its medieval incarnation, the 13th century royal residence in Buda, later a Habsburg prison where the two radical journalists Mihály Táncsics and Lajos Kossuth had been prisoners before the 1848 revolution. It now houses US marines working at the embassy!

In the Middle Ages, this was the main street of the Jewish ghetto which ran between here and Fortuna utca, down towards the city walls. Following the Tatar invasions of 1240-1 which decimated the fledgling city, King Béla IV brought Jewish, German and Italian settlers to the Castle Hill; each group was given a guarantee of its rights and the Jews were allowed to settle by Dísz tér. Growing anti-Jewish sentiments led to a series of restrictions on the Jewish community, who from 1279 were forced by the Buda Council to wear a red circle on their clothes as identification. In 1360, Lajos the Great expelled the Jews from Hungary but called them back four years later. In Buda, they were resettled here at the northern end of Castle Hill. Excavations in the 1960s, revealed remains of a medieval synagogue at No. 21-3, built in 1461, during the reign of King Mátyás, with a double nave and a prominent tower. No. 26 across the street, now the **Museum of the Medieval Synagogue**, was the house of the Jewish Prefect, an office created by King Mátyás and held by the Mendel family until 1539. The Prefect mediated between the Jewish community and the king, collected taxes, attended royal functions and was not obliged to wear the red circle. A small synagogue was also found in this house which is thought to have been used by the Syrian-Sephardic community. After the Battle of Mohács in 1526, when the Turks invaded central Hungary, the Jews were forced to flee from Buda, but were invited back by the Sultan in 1541. The damaged synagogue was repaired and the Jewish community began to flourish. In 1686, following the liberation of Buda by the united armies of Christendom under Habsburg leadership, the Jews were massacred. The museum contains the remains of both synagogues, a collection of religious artifacts, and tombstones found in an old Jewish cemetery.

Táncsics Mihály utca ends at the **Bécsi kapu tér** where Baroque harmony is interrupted by a mish-mash of styles, from the plain white Lutheran church and the stuccoed Rococo facades, to the excessive but somber grandeur of the **State Archives** and the solid Vienna Gate, rebuilt in 1936 as part of the celebrations to commemorate the 250th anniversary of Buda's liberation from the Turks. From the top of the Gate a small path follows the Anjou Bastion wall around the back of the archives. The small **turban-topped tomb** standing by the wall is that of the last Turkish governor, Abdurrahman Abdi Arnaut Pasha, who was killed at the age of 70 defending Buda against the Habsburg-led onslaught in

A golden yellow Baroque facade in Táncsics Mihály utca.

*One of many cannons
outside the Museum of
Military History.*

*The Museum's facade is
dotted with carefully
implanted cannon balls.*

1686. The monument was erected in 1932 by the family of a
Hungarian soldier, György Szabó, who was killed on this spot on the
day of liberation, as a symbol of reconciliation. The inscription
records, "He was a heroic enemy, let him rest in peace". Solemn
rows of cannons line the bastion beside the enormous Habsburg-
yellow **Military History Museum** (Hadtörténeti Múzeum), originally
built as a barracks in the 1830s. On the front facade, carefully
implanted cannon balls randomly dot the wall, in commemoration of
the brief Hungarian liberation of Buda Castle in 1849. Alongside the
usual patriotic blood and gore, the museum has a very interesting
new permanent exhibition, reconstructing the events of the 1956
revolution. One of the more fascinating exhibits is a huge hand of
Stalin from the statue that was toppled on the first day of the
October uprising.
Around the other side of the museum is Kapisztrán tér, named after
the statue of the Franciscan Papal Nuncio, John Capistrano, who
fought with János Hunyadi in the victorious anti-Turk Battle of
Belgrade in 1456. The statue is a ferocious depiction of the wild-eyed
monk towering over a Turk, defined in traditional style by his long

The sparse remains of the Magdalene Church.

pony-tail falling backwards to the ground in his agonies of death. But the dominant feature of the square is the lonely Gothic tower of the **Magdalene Church**. Built in 1276, this was the parish church of the Hungarian community. The Turks, having turned the more powerful Germans' Mátyás church into a mosque, forced the two communities to worship together. Several decades later, the church became the Victory Mosque. In 1945, all but the tower was completely destroyed. The tall Gothic window at the far end of the empty nave was added recently, adding a spatial dimension to the melancholy of the tower. From Országház utca, the perspective looking back at the tower is stunning.

Three streets run up towards the Mátyás church from Kapisztrán tér, all ideal for aimless wandering in the medieval and Baroque world of the Castle Hill. The houses Nos. 18, 20 and 22 on Országház utca are remarkable for their outspokenly Gothic features: large arched doorways, iron grilles and protruding windows, stemming from the 14th and 15th centuries. At the end of Fortuna köz (the alley to the left), the corner house on Fortuna utca 4 is home to the **Museum of Commerce and Catering** (Kereskedelmi és Vendéglátóipari Múzeum),

*A Gothic facade on
Országház utca.*

situated on either side of the inner courtyard. Despite the
unpromising name, the museum is well worth visiting. The catering
exhibition is a nostalgic journey back to the heyday of the
confectioner's world. Pervaded by the pungent aroma of sweet
vanilla, the museum displays everything from ornate rolling-pins to
fading photographs of proud coffee-house owners standing outside
their famous institutions. Across the courtyard, the commerce section
concentrates on old poster advertisements and rebuilt shop-fronts.
The taped information is now a period-piece in itself, describing in
good communist style the contradictory development of capitalist
trade from its feudal origins to the emergence of socialism, which
appears to require no explanation. The curator takes more pride in
the ornate cash register from Ohio and the little shop-front toy dog
which, at the flick of a switch, taps on the window to attract the
attention of passing shoppers.

The post-war renovation of Castle Hill uncovered a peculiarly
Hungarian contribution to Gothic architecture, the **sedilia**. These
arched niches lining the entrance-way can best be seen on Úri utca
(which you can reach by returning to Országház utca and then taking
Dárda utca to the right). Almost every house on this street has
sedilia. The best are in Nos. 42, 31, 34, and 32. The pointed arches
exude an oddly religious feel, but their function is thought to have
been more prosaic. Some believe the sedilia were used for displaying
wares, others that servants waited here for their masters to complete
their business inside. Another version is that they were simply the
rage, anybody who was anybody had sedilia. The steep steps at No. 9
lead down into the catacombs of Castle Hill, built by the Turks and
now housing a rather bad waxwork (or rather plastic-work) museum.
Úri utca leads back into Dísz tér. From here take the street to the
left of the Ministry of Defence which emerges at Szent György tér.

*Right
Gothic sedilia in Úri utca.*

The Royal Palace viewed from Pest.

This forlorn area between the peaceful streets of Castle Hill and the pompous neo-Baroque **Royal Palace** has proved a difficult task for the renovators. Controversy rages over the future of the blackened ministry ruins. The original eclectic domed building was of insufficient architectural value to justify rebuilding; but its site, where in the Middle Ages the executioner performed his bloody duty, has been too closely associated with violence and destruction to house a less somber building. Similar problems exist with how to use the newly renovated **Sándor Palace**, next to the theater (Várszínház). This used to be the prime ministerial residence and it was here that Admiral Horthy's prime minister, Pál Teleki, shot himself in April 1941 in protest at Hungary's decision to join the German attack on Yugoslavia, less than four months after signing a "Treaty of Eternal Friendship". The significance of his suicide remains an issue in Hungary, since the decision to join the war was a logical consequence of Teleki's efforts to regain the vast Hungarian territories lost in the Treaty of Trianon (1920), a subject that still rouses strong emotion in every Hungarian soul. The beautiful neo-Classical building now stands empty, waiting for a decision.

Having crossed this strange no-man's land, taken over by groups of tourists emerging from the funicular station, it is a relief to escape into the solid walls of the **Royal Palace** (Várpalota), now a complex of museums. The wrought iron gateway, topped by the almost audibly screeching "turul", a mythical bird said to have sired the father of the Magyar chief Árpád, is predictably a late 19th century creation. This part of the castle was rebuilt for Franz Joseph, following the destruction of 1849 and the Compromise of 1868, by Budapest's top conservative architects, Miklós Ybl and Alajos Hauszmann. The terrace here, with its proud equestrian statue of Eugene of Savoy, the famous Austrian general who took part in the liberation of Buda from the Turks, is best seen in the evening, when the lights of the parliament and the Chain Bridge down below are complemented by the gentle illumination of the palace.

Behind the statue is the entrance to the **National Gallery** (Nemzetí Galéria). The attraction of these paintings is not so much their artistic value as the insight they give into the Hungarian sense of identity. Hungary's history is marked by spectacular defeats and pyrric victories which have left a paradoxical combination of romantic nationalism and fatalism, a proud sense of isolation from the world and a striving to be an integral part of Western culture. These tensions are evident in Hungary's music, its architecture and, very clearly here, in its painting. The walls of the gallery bristle with lurid depictions of battles, rebellions, and betrayals; but also with softer, back-to-the roots images of life on the puszta, Hungary's great plain. Most of the artists are little known outside of Hungary; among the best are Mihály Munkácsy (famous through Europe in the late 19th century), Károly Lotz and Bertalan Székely (who worked on the Mátyás church), József Rippl-Ronai (influenced by Klimt) and Tivadar Csontváry-Kosztka (whose unusual paintings have something disconcertingly new-age about them). On the ground-floor there is a good collection of medieval altar paintings and on the very top floor a display of the best of Hungary's modern painters.

The gateway to the Royal Palace, with the turul statue.

Peter Krafft - Zriny's Retreat, 1825 (National Gallery).

Mihály Munkácsy - Dusty Road, 1874 (National Gallery)

*Right
Gyula Benczur - The Baptism of Vajk, 1875 (National Gallery)*

The Royal Palace from Tabán.

Walk through the passageway into the inner courtyard. The building on the right houses the **Museum of Contemporary History** (Legújabbkori Történeti Múzeum), a very successful reorientation of what was until 1990 the obligatory East bloc homage to the labour movement. The only permanent exhibition is the Ludwig Collection, a gallery of 70 post-war paintings collected by Irene and Peter Ludwig (German chocolate-factory owners!), concentrating on Hungarian works but including several Picassos. The real attraction of the place, especially for Hungarians, is the temporary exhibitions which tend to focus on the communist past with a sense of humour and originality of presentation that is startling.

Before continuing into the next courtyard, take a closer look at the **fountain** on the corner. The subject is taken from a ballad by the romantic 19th century poet, Mihály Vörösmarty, in which King Mátyás meets the beautiful Ilonka while out hunting. It is the naturalistic details that make Alajos Stróbl's rendering of the tale so compelling: the panting hounds, the fallen stag and the cool skepticism of the court poet who realises the impossibility of love between a lowly noblewoman and a king. The fountain was erected in 1904, at the same time as the lions guarding the inner courtyard — two merely haughty, the other two positively ferocious. From here, with some help from the **Budapest History Museum** (Budapesti Történeti Múzeum) at the back of the courtyard, we can start to peel off the layers of the Royal Palace.

The Baroque buildings to the left were erected as a royal residence for Empress Maria Theresa in 1715-1738. But underneath this whole area lie five centuries of royal palace remains. The first palace, more a military fortress than a residence, was built by Béla IV in 1243, to defend Buda against further Tatar invasions. In the 1350s, the Anjou kings, starting with Lajos the Great, began to build a royal court here. The coloured contours on the courtyard floor trace the ground plan of this palace. The next king was Sigismund of Luxemburg, also king of Bohemia and, after 1433, Holy Roman Emperor, whose grandiose ambitions warranted a multi-storey Gothic complex, with moats and dungeons, gardens and towers, known as the "Fresh Palace". King Mátyás, under the aesthetic influence of his wife Beatrix of Naples, gave a strong Renaissance accent to the palace and turned it into a humanist haven, with the glorious Bibliotheca Corvina, craft workshops and music halls. The invading Turks were reportedly highly impressed by the red marble interiors, golden ceilings and mosaic floors of the palace, but during their occupation of Buda used it as a barracks. One of the humanist scholars who had visited the palace during its heyday, described the consequences of occupation in 1553: "the ornate halls and rooms have been divided into dirty compartments, and the stench and filth spoil everything". What remained of its glory was destroyed by the Habsburg-led attack which finally ousted the Turks in 1686. According to a contemporary account, "the Palace looked like an empty skull with a candle burning inside". In the early 1700s, the ruins were flattened and the rubble used to raise the area to the height of the surrounding walls. It was on this surface that the Habsburgs built their Baroque palace. As with the Mátyás Church, the destruction and rebuilding

The Lion Gateway looking into Szt. György tér.

continued: destroyed in 1849, and rebuilt as a luxury residence in the 1890s, it was badly damaged in 1945 and finally rebuilt as a museum complex.

The post-war rebuilding was combined with intensive archaeological work (still continuing) to uncover the remains of the Gothic and Renaissance structures. The results form the core of the History Museum. Down the steps from the ground floor, the rooms plunge into the depths of the medieval castle. The rooms lead through a smoke-blackened cellar into a high-ceilinged dungeon, used by King László V to imprison the popular Mátyás Corvinus in 1457; when Mátyás became king in 1458, he used the rooms to imprison the notorious killer, Vlad Tepes the Impaler more commonly known as Dracula. The most magnificent rooms in the museum are from an earlier era. The spacious cross-vaulted **Gothic Hall** is from Sigismund's Palace (early 15th century) and is now used to display a

collection of limestone Gothic statues from the same time, uncovered in 1974. It appears that the statues were tossed into a pit in the palace grounds during one of the reconstructions, breaking off heads, arms and noses, but preserving the works of art from almost certain destruction. The tiny atmospheric **Royal Chapel** was built during the reign of the Anjou kings in the 14th century; it miraculously survived the subsequent reconstructions and sieges, and was uncovered more or less intact in the 1960s. It was reconsecrated as an ecumenical chapel in 1990.

Leave by the doors opposite the main entrance which lead to the Ferdinand Gate and the Mace Tower, past the Southern Bastion, and down a wide grassy slope, with wonderful views of the liberation monument on Gellért Hill, down into the houses of Tabán. About halfway down on the left, under the protective branches of a few trees, is a scattering of small higgeldy-piggeldy posts topped with

The mace Tower on the southern walls of the Royal Palace.

Left
The Royal Chapel in the Budapest History Museum.

The head of a knight, one of the Gothic statues discovered in 1974.

37

Turban-topped graves in the tiny Turkish cemetery.

turbans — the peaceful remains of an old **Turkish graveyard**. Walking around the church, we come into a park at the middle of the clover leaf junction that leads to the **Elizabeth Bridge**. Queen Elizabeth, murdered in 1896 by an Italian anarchist, sits here resplendently beautiful and unmoved by the ideological swings that shifted the statue in 1946 from its original site on the Pest side of the bridge, forcing it into obscurity for forty years until, it reappeared here in 1986. A plaque on the ground commemorates the ideologically inspired fate of yet another statue: this was the location during the Horthy regime of a statue to Gyula Gömbös, initiator of the inter-war pro-German policy; the statue was blown up in October 1944 as the communist front's first act of resistance.

Behind it runs the sleek modern lines of the Elizabeth bridge, the only one to have been completely remodelled after the destruction of 1945. During the construction of the original bridge at the turn of the century, a hot spring was mistakenly opened up in the river bed, drastically reducing the water supply to all the thermal baths. After several unsuccessful attempts and with the growing unease of the large bathing community, the spring was finally sealed. The bridge crosses to Felszabadulás tér, close to Váci utca.

PEST INNER CITY

Until the 19th century, the city of Pest was entirely overshadowed by Buda. Smaller in population and cramped by its still existing medieval walls, Pest was a market town of around 20,000 people. In the 1800s, the situation changed drastically. Flooded by peasants and immigrants, Pest burst out of its walls, began to assert its growing national and civic pride in a spate of monumental buildings, and by the end of the century was caught up in a commercial and cultural frenzy that turned the capital into an integral part of Europe. From the creation of the Dual Monarchy in 1867 and the unification of Buda, Pest and Óbuda in 1872, to the First World War, Budapest was the throbbing heart of a vast country. That it was still second to Vienna and under Habsburg rule only quickened the nationalistic beat; and that internal tensions were slowly coming to boiling point only intensified the drama. It was these heady years that shaped Pest, giving the city a cosmopolitan appearance and energetic atmosphere that none of the disasters of the 20th century was able to suppress.

The **Parliament** (Országház) is both spiritually and architecturally an embodiment of the aspirations of this era. Construction began in 1885 and continued for 17 years, under the personal direction of architect Imre Steidl who died shortly before the doors opened in 1902. Stretching its medieval pinnacles along the Danube, and rising to an elegant Renaissance dome topped by a sharp Gothic spire, the building captures the adventurous possibilities of eclecticism. Prime Minister Kálmán Tísza was adamant about the building's symbolic importance; its 691 rooms, 27 entrances and 41 kilos of 24-carat gold were intended, he declared, to impress "the eyes of our friends and foes alike". At home, the enormous costs were a subject of substantial controversy, but other critics were more concerned with the substance of the symbol. One wondered whether there would ever be sufficient democracy in Hungary to fill such a space. Sadly, until the last few years, the answer has been a very clear no. Except for the few chaotic months of the Hungarian Republic under Mihály Károlyi in 1918-19, and the year or two of threatened democracy after 1945, Parliament was the home of the rubber-stamp, with real power always located elsewhere. During the communist era, the red star perched on the dome was a constant reminder of the institution's impotence. But it was here that thousands of citizens gathered to force parliament to vote for the first time against the government in summer 1989; and it was from the balcony on Kossuth tér that the end of the Hungarian People's Republic was

*A wintry view of
Parliament over the roofs of
Buda.*

announced a few months later. The red star was taken down in 1990,
marking the revival of democracy in Hungary. The spectacular
interior can only be visited in a group, organized by Ibusz offices or
any hotel.

Parliament opens on to **Kossuth Lajos tér**, named after the
revolutionary leader of 1848. His statue on the square could easily be
mistaken for a memorial to Soviet power, and indeed the original
gentle white marble monument to his defeat was replaced during the
Stalinist era by this glorification of blind optimism, predictably a
work of the master of authoritarian sculpture, Zsigmond Kisfaludi
Stróbl. These two extremes — melancholy identification with tragedy
and strutting patriotism — compete with each other in Hungarian
statuary and perhaps in the Hungarian soul. The melancholy side is
beautifully represented in two statues on either side of parliament.
To the north in a small park stands the sad stooped figure of Mihály
Károlyi under a broken pointed arch, representing his leadership of
the short-lived democratic parliament (Imre Várga, 1975). Károlyi
escaped to Paris in 1919 during Béla Kun's Council Republic. After
the war he was Hungarian ambassador in France, but he fell into
disfavour for his criticism of the Stalinist show-trials. In 1962, seven
years after his death, the communists rehabilitated Károlyi and
reburied him in style in the prestigious Kerepesi Cemetery. To the
south is the brooding presence of the poet, Attila József, looking out

over the Danube. This Orwellian figure threw himself under a train in 1937 at the age of 32 in despair at the direction Hungary's authoritarian government was taking.

The pompous facade of the **Ethnographic Museum** (Néprajzi Múzeum) across from the Parliament, originally the Palace of Justice, bears no traces of this collective awareness of tragedy. The plans for the building won second place for architect. Alajos Hauszmann, to Imre Steidl's winning submission in the 1880 competition held to choose a suitable parliament. This may explain its distinct resemblance to the Berlin Reichstag. In a fit of civic magnanimity, the government decided to make use of the top three prize-winners; the Agricultural Ministry across the road came third. The museum's permanent exhibition runs through different facets of traditional Hungarian life — youth to old age, celebrations marking the religious and agricultural year, the development of housing and so on. But even those not interested in such things should buy a ticket just to be able to walk around the breathtaking interior, a marvel of eclecticism with its red and black marble pillars, white stairways, stained glass windows and huge gilded ceiling painting by Károly Lotz.

Walk down the monumental Alkotmány utca, turning right on to Hold utca which until 1991 bore the bulky name, Rosenberg Couple Street, designed to shame the Americans whose embassy backs on to

Parliament in all its glory, but topped by a red star.

The gilded dome of Parliament.

*Right
Hauszmann's spectacular
entrance hall in the
Ethnographic Museum.*

*Justice rides on top of the
Ethnographic Museum,
Formerly the Supreme
Court.*

the street. On the corner with Báthory utca, in the centre of the junction, stands a tiny **eternal flame** enclosed in a sober casket and dedicated to the memory of Count Lajos Batthyány, Prime Minister of the Revolutionary Government 1848-9, who was killed by firing squad here in October 1849. At that time, the junction was a corner courtyard of a vast Habsburg military barracks, built in 1786 during the centralizing drive of Emperor Joseph II and still known as New Building. This symbol of oppression was ceremoniously demolished in 1897. Most of the area was incorporated into **Szabadság tér** (Freedom Square), a peaceful tree-filled oasis that was soon transformed into a showcase of turn-of-the-century affluence. But its significance as the site of national mourning and rebirth has never been forgotten. During the Horthy era, it was the focus of public grief over the huge pieces of territory lost in the 1920 Treaty of Trianon. A statue stood in each of the four tiny lawns at the top of the square, representing the land lost to Slovakia, Romania, Yugoslavia and Austria; in the centre a flag flew permanently at half-mast, expressing the regime's refusal to accept the new borders. After the war, the flag was taken away and replaced with a bulky monument to the Soviet liberation. Now that the liberators have finally left Hungary, debate is raging once again on how to deal with this sacred spot. Meanwhile, one of the old statues has been dusted down and reerected in its former position; this is dedicated to Harry Hill Bandholz, an American general who prevented the crown jewels from falling into Romanian hands in 1919. The plaque notes that the statue was erected in 1936, taken down in 1949 and returned in 1989!

The buildings surrounding Szabadság tér are a fascinating record of the transition from eclecticism to art nouveau, the former taking its inspiration from the past, the latter seeking to express the spirit of the age. The four blocks around the semi-circular top of the square appear at first glance as a harmonious unit, but each building has its own historicist concept. No. 16 bristles with seafaring details, from boats and waves, to shells, anchors and chains, appropriate to its original owners, the Hungarian Shipping Company. Above the ridged pillars of No. 15, the classical tympanum tells the story of Count Wesselényi's rescue mission during the great flood of 1838 which destroyed much of old Pest. The enormous white pillared and turreted bulk of the TV centre, running down the side of the square, used to be the Stock Exchange, its indigestible mixture of forms marking the worst of eclecticism's waning years. The **National Bank** on the corner already has some lighter art nouveau touches, with its wonderful sculpted faces from around the world. The middle block (1899-1901), housing the **American Embassy** and two apartment buildings, stands out in its art nouveau simplicity. Taking inspiration from the Viennese secessionists, the architects Geza Kármán and Gyúla Ullmann brought the plain lines to life with sinuous details. But the real jewel of Hungarian art nouveau is behind this block on Hold utca. This is Ödön Lechner's wildly ornate and colourful **Post Office Bank** (Postatakarékpénztar) completed in 1901. **Lechner's** ambition was to create a peculiarly Hungarian style of architecture by integrating folk art and Eastern influences into the refined world of

European culture. The facade is a joyous experimentation of textures and shapes, combining brick with mosaic and ceramics, erect pillars with delicately curved window frames and an undulating serpentine roof. Lechner placed his architectonic emphasis on the roof which is a riot of coloured tiles and playful details — bees climbing up the pillars to yellow ceramic bee-hives, an octopus-like crown, and a central tower decorated with a bull's head motif which represented the popular belief at the time in a link between the Huns and the Hungarians. The banking hall (open on weekday mornings) is a curvaceous fantasy of yellow and white floral patterns. This spurt of creativity aroused intense criticism from Lechner's colleagues and he completed only three public buildings in his unique child-like style. The architect's reaction was calm; when asked why he focused on roof details which nobody could see, he commented, "the birds will see them."

From Lechner's excesses the solidity and urbanity of **St. Stephen's Basilica**, a five-minute walk down Alpári Gyúla utca, is a sobering experience. The Basilica (referring to its status rather than its shape) was started in 1851 by the ageing József Hild; in 1886 after his death Miklós Ybl took over and was horrified to discover cracks in the walls. A few days later, the enormous dome collapsed, and Ybl was faced with a major reworking of the original plans. The dome was not the only problem; since work began, Pest had developed a system of ring-roads, one of which swept grandly past the insignificant back of the church. Ybl neatly solved the problem with

Lechner's playful roof on the Post Office Savings Bank.

Left
A wrought iron gateway in Kossuth Lajos tér.

Lechner's tower has an octopus-like form.

45

The back of St. Stephen's Basilica, with the apostles looking out on to Bajcsy Zsilinszky út.

One of the side domes on St. Stephen's Basilica.

a semi-circular colonnade, topped with statues. He died in 1891 leaving the last phase of construction to József Kauser, who finally brought the mammoth project to an end in 1906. The shadowy interior is more suited to prayer than sight-seeing, but at certain times of day, narrow rays of golden light stream through the tiny windows and lend an eerie mystery to the place, compounded by the ghostly white statue of King István I behind the altar. In a small chapel (Szt. Jobb Kápolna) at the back of the church, the strangeness continues; there in a gold and glass casket and wrapped in jewels is the **Holy Dexter**, St. István's right hand curled into a fist, as the curator will ghoulishly demonstrate for those who put a coin in the slot. The Holy Dexter (as befits an object with such a name) has had an eventful life, leaving István's arm at his death in 1038, enjoying a popularity boost with his canonisation in 1083, and then moving from one area of the Habsburg Empire to another until returning to Hungary in 1945. Every year on St. István's day, August 20, the Holy Dexter (or St. Right in literal translation) is paraded around the streets of Budapest. The chapel pays homage with its stained glass windows to the Árpád dynasty; opposite, are old photographs recording the building of the Basilica, including one of the collapsed dome.

It is a straight shot down Zrínyi utca to Roosevelt tér and it's worth looking back to catch this unobtrusive axis, with its appealing glimpse of the church's urban grandeur. It was in this square, under its former name, Ferenc József tér, that the Austrian emperor sealed his 1867 agreement with the Hungarian nation; sitting astride his horse, the strange Hungarian crown with its crooked cross and hanging jewels perched precariously on his head, Franz Joseph swore to protect Hungary from its enemies, marking the points of the compass with the heavy coronation sword. Nowadays, Roosevelt tér is so ringed with traffic that it is difficult to find a peaceful spot from which to appreciate its numerous charms.

Easily the most stunning is the huge gold-trimmed art nouveau **Gresham Palace** at No. 5, built in 1905 by Zsigmond Quittner for the London-based insurance company. The glass-domed interior, housing fusty offices and ageing apartments, has clearly seen better days. But it is the careful details that give the palace its appeal: the wrought iron gates looking directly on to the Chain Bridge through swirls of peacocks, the intricate mosaics, tiled hallways and benches. At the center of the glittering facade, the casual observer remembering the era of red stars might be forgiven for seeing the

The 96-metre high central dome of St. Stephen's Basilica.

47

Wrought-iron peacocks on the Gresham Palace gate.

image of Lenin in a flat cap; it is in fact Lord Gresham, founder of the London Stock Exchange. Ignore as far as possible the sickly green monstrosity known to Hungarians as the "spinach barracks", and take a look at No.9, along the side of the square. This is the **Hungarian Academy of Science** (Magyar Tudományos Akadémia), built like the Chain Bridge on the initiative of Count Széchenyi, who sacrificed a year's salary to spur fund-raising for the building. When asked how he was going to survive for the year, the count is said to have replied, "I have friends"! Completed in 1864, it was the first neo-Renaissance building in Budapest, and the first of many monumental tributes to Hungary's growing sense of national importance. István Széchenyi's statue stands in the park across from the rather more sober seated figure of Ferenc Deák, the architect of the 1867 Compromise.

The **Dunakorzó** (promenade) running along the Danube from Roosevelt tér was once lined with magnificent hotels, the Bristol, the Carlton and the Ritz, and bustled with music, cafes and strollers. The destruction of 1945 and the requirements of public transport have brought a more mundane feel to the walkway. But if we turn away from the disappointing blocks of the Forum and Intercontinental and ignore the trundling yellow trams, the view is both intimate and overpowering. The dramatic outlines of the Palace and the Mátyás Church rise high above the relentless flow of the Danube, tamed only by the solid towers and seductive curves of the Chain Bridge. The view changes throughout the day and with every season as mists and shadows alter the perspective; at night, the sharp contours dissolve into flood-lit silhouette and the bridge loops across the water like a sparkling necklace. In an attempt to revive the leisurely tradition of the promenade, the city-fathers have brought back the "Buchwald" chairs, rows of individual wood and wrought-iron armchairs, that used to cost a small sum to rent, turning the ingenious Mr. Buchwald into a millionaire.

The pontoon bridge that served for centuries as the only link between Buda and Pest, was moored at the point where the promenade opens out into Vigadó tér. The solid neo-Renaissance corner building gives a glimpse of how the rows of hotels must have looked. One innovation that does not hark back to older traditions is the little statue of a court jester, sitting on the rails as if waiting for tram no. 2 with everybody else. The square is defined by the romantic extravagance of the **Vigadó** concert hall, built in 1865 by Frigyes Feszl. Playing on Goethe's remark that architecture is frozen music, one German architect called the building "crystallized csárdás", after the wild and haunting gypsy music that accompanies many a meal in Budapest. Feszl, like Lechner a few decades later, was trying to create a peculiarly Hungarian style, combining Eastern influence with Hungarian and Western elements. The effect is provocative if only because the incomplete synthesis leaves the eye darting from turret to statue to arch. The frieze of busts running above the windows reads like a quick course in Hungarian history, combining the three favoured Habsburgs, Maria Theresa, Palatine Joseph and Elizabeth, with the best of the Hungarian kings, the odd non-royal hero such as Széchenyi and, for good measure, Attila the

Right
The art nouveau facade of the Gresham Palace.

The Danube corso in summer.

Right
Buchwald chairs on the Danube corso.

Trams run along the length of the Danube corso.

Hun, to emphasize Hungary's Eastern connections. The ornate interior can only be seen during a concert, but you can get a glimpse of the stairway from the ticket hall which is open in the afternoon. Vigadó utca, to the left of the hall, runs straight into **Vörösmarty tér**, the main meeting point of Pest. Its main claim to fame is the **Gerbeaud coffee-house**, founded here in 1870 and taken over by Emile Gerbeaud of Geneva in 1884. At this time there were some 600 luxurious cafes in Budapest, each catering to a loyal and distinct clientele for whom the place was a second home or office from where to do business, write poetry, read the international press or deal with correspondence. Gerbeaud has preserved something of the atmosphere of this era, complete with heavy wallpaper, art nouveau

marble tables, delicious cakes and ageing dowagers. Bút its survival as an island of bourgeois nostalgia, miraculously maintained through the communist era (despite an official name-change until 1984), is now endangered by floods of tourists. In front of the cafe is the end-station of the "little metro", a tiny train running a few meters underground up the length of Andrássy út to Heroes' Square and beyond. At its opening during the Millennial celebrations of 1896, it was the first underground railway on the continent.

The square is named after the **statue of Mihály Vörösmarty**, the 19th century romantic poet, surrounded by 24 figures reciting his (memorable?) line, "Be faithful to your land forever, Oh Hungarians", carved into the pedestal. Sculpted in delicate Carrara

Page 53
The Vigadó concert hall looking out over the Danube.

The Vörösmarty statue wrapped for winter; behind it, the Luxus department store by Giergl and Korb.

marble, the statue is draped in protective plastic in winter, giving this most conservative of monuments the look of an experimental "happening". The graciousness of this public space, enlivened by portrait artists and musicians, gains much from the restrained art nouveau beauty of the **Luxus** department store, built in 1911 by Kálmán Giergl and Floris Korb, who added several gems to Budapest's rich collection of turn-of-the-century architecture. The modern building opposite adds nothing to the atmosphere but houses the excellent Hungaroton record shop and the central ticket office for classical concerts.

Váci utca, Hungary's equivalent of the ubiquitous European pedestrian shopping street, runs off Vörösmarty tér, becoming a frenetic mix of elegant brand-name stores, rounded peasant women selling their colourful folk art with an eye out for passing policemen, shifty money-changers, and walking advertisements for the latest peep-shows. Among the bustle of the best and worst of Hungary's enthusiastic embrace of capitalism, the eye catches a glimpse of an art nouveau detail, a wooden store-front, a meeting of two post-modern facades, an interesting antiquarian bookshop, only to plunge back into the world of McDonalds and street-vendors. Behind Váci

Vörösmarty tér is a central meeting-point in Pest.

utca, through one of the alleys to the left, is **Martinelli tér**.
The discordant square juxtaposes styles with criminal abandon, but among the chaos a tall thin art nouveau facade stands out with its glinting mosaic. Built in 1906 this used to be the **Török Banking House**.

Back on Váci utca, take Régi posta utca past McDonalds (the very first to be set up in Eastern Europe and for a time the most profitable in the world) to emerge at Petőfi tér by the Danube. Inconspicuously nestled among houses is the crippled Greek Orthodox Church, its second tower having been destroyed in the war. Here in a little park stands the statue of revolutionary poet **Sándor Petőfi,** scroll in raised hand, proclaiming his rousing verse to the receptive Hungarian ear of March 15, 1848: "Arise, Magyars. Your fatherland calls/This is the time, it's now or never/Do we want to be captives or free men?/This is the question, answer it!" And answer they did, rushing out from Cafe Pilvax in the pouring rain to rouse the masses.

Lajos Kossuth sent a delegation to Vienna where the doddering emperor granted their twelve demands. But they didn't remain free for long: Petőfi was killed at the age of 26 in Transylvania during the Habsburg counter-attack of 1849, Kossuth went into life-long exile in Torino, sixteen leading generals, including Batthyány, were executed and the remaining leaders were shackled in New Building barracks.

The relevance and insurrectionary appeal of Petőfi's words never lost their meaning for Hungarians. Next to the statue, on **Március 15 tér**, the citizens of Budapest have gathered in times of trouble and rebellion, strengthening their resolve with historical pathos. On March 15, 1942, opponents of Admiral Horthy's increasingly pro-Nazi policy organized a huge anti-war demonstration here. On October 23, 1956, students gathered at the statue and, after hearing an actor read Petőfi's verse, demanded free elections, the withdrawal of Soviet troops and the resignation of Stalinist party chief, Mátyás Rákosi. This was the spark that led to revolution. Hundreds of thousands of people joined the students. Some toppled the Stalin statue near Heroes' Square, others went to the radio station to broadcast their demands. For almost two weeks, the revolution looked like it might be a success. Rákosi was spirited away to the Soviet Union, allowing the popular reformist, Imre Nagy, to become prime minister, and Hungary was caught up in a wave of democracy. By November 4, the Soviets had decided the situation was too dangerous. They sent in troops, imprisoned and later executed the leaders of the revolution, and installed János Kádár as party chief. Március 15 tér looks like an unlikely place for revolution. Its large formless grassy plain drops into a rather sorry-looking sunken garden that holds the remains of the Roman outpost of **Contra Acquincum**. It takes a powerful imagination to recreate from the scant walls the huge fortress that stood here in the third century defending the Roman province of Pannonia and the settlement of Aquincum across the river in what is now Óbuda. At one time, it was even visited by Emperors Constantine the Great and Julian the Apostate — but that is really beyond comprehension.

The art nouveau facade of the former Török Banking House on Martinelli tér.

The declamatory statue of Sándor Petöfi, looking out on to the towers of the Parish Church.

Across the square is the **Inner City Parish Church** (Belvárosi Plébániatemplom), its glory as the oldest building in Pest eclipsed by the immense bridge-head skirting round its nave, and its age concealed by the curves of its rather ordinary yellow Baroque facade. The church's history is a bizarre catalogue of religious urgings and military defeats. Following the burial of the martyred Bishop Gellért here in 1046, the victorious Christian kings erected a large Romanesque church. Only experts can identify the few stones left from this era, but the Gothic rebuilding necessitated after the devastating Tatar invasion is still clearly visible. Take a good look at the church from the side. The Baroque facade was added in 1739 as the church was rebuilt and reconsecrated after doing time as a mosque during the Turkish occupation, but this suddenly fades into a darker medieval stone, interspersed with Gothic pointed windows and buttresses. Inside, the atmosphere is neither Baroque nor Gothic. The church bursts with light and colour — a very peaceful space of human dimensions. On either side of the church at the end of the aisles are two red marble Renaissance tabernacles dating from 1507, as well as fragments of medieval frescoes. Among the nineteen Gothic sedilia behind the altar is a rare reminder of the Turkish

occupation (1541-1686), a mihrab or prayer niche, identifiable by its flowing Arabic calligraphy spelling out the name of Allah.

The **Parish Church** used to be at the very heart of the walled city of Pest and was surrounded by a sumptuous collection of 18th century buildings. The diminutive Baroque **Péterffy Palace** on the corner with Pesti Barnabós utca is the only surviving dwelling from this era. The dismantling of this Baroque and classical oasis began gradually. The great flood of 1838 damaged two-thirds of the buildings, the fighting of 1848-9 destroyed others and the influx of population broke down the city walls, expanding the city outward. In the 1870s, planners reoriented the city's infrastructure around two major ring-roads, the smaller one, following the old walls from what is now Szabadság bridge to Deák tér. The grand finale came at the turn of the century, with the building of the **Erzsébet Bridge** (1897-1903). Its huge dimensions required the razing of numerous buildings. The architects had originally planned to pull down the Parish Church itself, but were finally forced to snake the road around it. The large faceless building behind the church, with its imposing archway leading through to Váci utca, took the place of the 18th century **Old City Hall**. Originally a Piarist monastery (their 18th century site had also

The Inner City Parish Church and university buildings on Marcius 15 tér.

The wrought iron gateway to the Paris Arcade.

The serpentine road to the Elizabeth Bridge, skirting around the towers of the Parish Church.

Right
The Central Market Hall on Vamhaz körut.

fallen in the name of progress), the building now houses the University Faculty of Arts.

Across Váci utca, Kigyó utca emerges into the turn-of-the-century, but now traffic-filled, world created by the construction of the bridge. And despite our sighs for times past, this quintessential Budapest scene has an energy and monumentalism that is invigorating. Immediately to the left on **Felszabadulás tér** (Liberation Square, at its creation in 1900, Serpent Sq.) is the **Paris Arcade** (Párisi udvar), a marvellous high-ceilinged passageway with Venetian-

style balconies and dappled light falling through broken stained glass windows and wrought iron gates. Erected in 1911 by Henrik Schmahl, the huge building is a bristling but elegant mixture of neo-Gothic and art nouveau. In a stroke of genius, the Luxus duo, Giergl and Korb, built in 1902 two narrow mirror-image palaces, the **Klotild palota**, functioning like a gateway to focus the eye on the bridge's fine axis. Just up the road, the Baroque facade of the Franciscan church — a powder-room pink and blue inside — is a reminder of old Pest. The relief on the side portrays (once again) Wesselényi's heroic relief efforts during the 1838 flood.

Down towards the river, Váci utca continues on the other side of Erzsébet Bridge, cutting through towards the ring-road at Vámház körút. The tourist traffic abated, this side of Váci utca presents a less hectic and more residential face, interspersed with tiny stores selling buttons, stamps and old chairs. Across the ring-road from Váci utca is the **Central Market Hall** (Központi Vásárcsarnok), a marvel of 19th century brick and iron architecture, with splendid neo-Gothic towers and the feel of a grand station. In the 1890s, the Budapest council decided that the open markets were a health hazard, giving off ''the stench of the plague''. They decided to commission architect Samu Pecz to build five custom-designed glass-covered halls, all of which were opened on the same day in 1897. In this the largest, with space for 1100 stands, goods could be brought directly into the hall either by train on a special side-rail or by barge through a tunneled canal from the river. Inside, under the span of iron girders, the senses are bombarded in an intoxicating whirl of red peppers, fish, sauerkraut, garlic and beans. The Vámház körút leads into Szabadság Híd (Liberation Bridge), completed for the Millenium Celebrations in 1896.

Back on Váci utca, the narrow Szerb utca runs off to the right passing a sleepy walled garden. Here seemingly forgotten among the trees is the pale yellow **Serbian Orthodox Church**, at peace among the scattered graves. The Serbs were brought to Budapest in 1717. Their Patriarch had helped Eugene of Savoy in his Balkan battles against the Turks; when the Turks advanced again, the Patriarch and his 40,000 followers were offered refuge throughout the Habsburg Empire. At the top of the street, the corner house with Királyi Pál utca has a discreet but lovely monument to the great flood, erected in 1938 at the centenary. The flooded area is delineated in red marble on a white map of Budapest, and the water level reached is marked on the wall.

We are now on Egyetem tér, dominated by the neo-Baroque **Law and Political Science Faculties of the University**. But the real jewel is the **University Church** adjoining it around the corner. In a city with little of the soul-stirring sensuality that marks Counter-Reformation Baroque, this church comes as a welcome surprise. Its dynamic interior is a riot of wonderfully executed imitation marble and distorted perspective paintings, calmed by exquisite wood carving on the pulpits, doors and pews, the work of monks of the Pauline order. The Paulines, founded by Hungarians in the 13th century, had built their original church in a small town outside Budapest around relics of St. Paul acquired by King Lajos the Great (1342-82). This was

A tiled monument to St. George, outside the Serbian church.

Left
The peaceful icon-filled interior of the Serbian church.

The Liberation Bridge.

The turul-topped towers of the Liberation Bridge frame the liberation monument on Gellért Hill.

destroyed by Turks during the occupation. In satisfying revenge, the order moved to Pest in 1686, took over a Turkish mosque and had this church built in its place (which may explain why the chancel does not face eastwards). The church was consecrated in 1742. In 1786, during Joseph II's spring-cleaning drive, the order was abolished and its church given to the new University.

Across the road, Henszlmann utca runs up to Magyar utca where the inconspicuous doorway of No. 28 leads through an unpromising passageway into a courtyard. Here a section of castellated wall, pierced by arrow slits, emerges unexpectedly from the surrounding houses. This fairy-tale fragment is part of the original **medieval city wall**, built around Pest at the end of the 15th century. During the city's frenetic 19th century expansion, it gradually disappeared into the new buildings.

The courtyard emerges at Múzeum körút, across from the grand eight-pillared facade of the **National Museum** (Nemzeti Múzeum). The initial collection was donated to the nation in 1802 by Count Ferenc Széchenyi, the father of István Széchenyi, and housed in the Pauline monastery, next to the University church. Palatine Archduke Joseph, the king's regent and a fervent supporter of Hungary's national aspirations, bought this site, at that time a quiet area outside the city walls, and in 1836 commissioned the master of neo-Classical architecture, Mihály Pollack, to design the building.

Construction was interrupted by the great flood of 1838, but the building was ready in time for the revolution of 1848. Copies of Petőfi's rousing Magyar poem, freshly printed in defiance of censorship, were distributed to the crowds on its steps, thus inaugurating the new building more resolutely than any official ceremony. Some of the statues in the museum garden hark back to this time of international nationalism, with a peculiarly Italian slant. The bust of Alexander Monti commemorates the general who led the Italian legion during the Hungarian revolution, and the statue of Giuseppe Garibaldi is a reminder of the reverse favour, when Hungarians took part in the Italian 1849 struggle against Habsburg rule. The Italian connection was forged once again in 1930 with Benito Mussolini's gift to the Hungarian nation of a column from the Forum Romanum. From the back of the garden, an ornate iron fence is all that remains of the Festetich residence; it now guards the new

The columns of the National Museum.

radio station, scene of some of the heaviest fighting during the 1956 revolution.

The museum's most important exhibit is the **Hungarian crown jewels**, on the ground floor. The colourful enamelled crown topped by its unforgettable crooked cross, the sword, sceptre and orb, now sit peacefully on red velvet, surrounded by the delicate semi-circular coronation mantle and three ornate zinc crown jewel containers stemming from the coronation of Franz Joseph (1867), and the last royal rulers, Karl and Zita (1916). The symbolic importance of these objects goes far beyond their strange medieval beauty. They represent for Hungarians their inception as a European state in the year 1000, when Pope Sylvester II sent the crown to István, transforming him from a mere prince into the apostolic king of Hungary. One story tells that the cross was bent during the rocky journey from Rome to the coronation city of Esztergom; as a new Christian, István assumed that crooked crosses were the norm and proudly wore the crown as it was. Experts have proven that the crown cannot actually be István's original, but a welding together of two Byzantine crowns. But regardless of its origins, the crown soon became the fiercely courted symbol of legitimate rule. After the Turkish victory at the Battle of Mohács in 1526, the Sultan stole the crown and presented it to his ally, John Zapolya, ruler of Transylvania. At his death in 1551, his wife Isabella was forced to recognise the Habsburg succession but broke off the cross before handing the crown over to Ferdinand. During the long years of Habsburg rule, the crown shuttled backwards and forwards between Austria and Hungary (at some point being dropped, thus accounting for the cross); in 1849, the jewels disappeared for four years, having been buried by a loyal Hungarian in a Transylvanian ditch. Once recovered, the crown soon adorned the head of Franz Joseph and in 1916, for the last time, Emperor Karl. In the final days of the war, members of the retreating Nazi-supported Arrow Cross government took the jewels to Austria, where they persuaded a village priest to hide them in a cardboard box. The priest, rather worried about the ramifications, finally told an American general (who just happened to be of Hungarian origin) about his hidden treasure. The jewels disappeared once again until 1965, when the Americans admitted to holding the jewels in Fort Knox as the "property of the Hungarian people". After years of pressure from the determinedly non-royalist communist government, US Secretary of State Cyrus Vance returned the jewels to Budapest in 1978.

The top floor of the National Museum is devoted to Hungarian history from the "Taking of the Land" in 896 to the Revolution of 1848. The English descriptions are rather stilted (and still scarred by Marxist terminology), but some of the objects — a luxurious Turkish officer's tent from 1683, ornate carved pews, collections of pottery and furniture — are well worth a quick look.

Múzeum körút runs into the traffic-filled wasteland of Kálvin tér, a victim of war bombing, relieved only slightly by the severe white facade of the **Calvinist Church**. The sleepy courtyard at No. 9, formerly the Two Lions Inn (see above the doorway), gives an idea of how the square used to look in the early 18th century. The

The crooked cross of St. Stephen's Crown, piercing the heart of Christ.

St. Stephen's Crown, with the Byzantine Emperor Michael Ducas in the centre.

The coronation sceptre, with the silver lion and golden bells.

Stained glass ceiling window in the Museum of Applied Arts.

contemplative statue seemingly abandoned among the shrubs is part of the original Danubius fountain that used to stand in the middle of the square; badly damaged in the last war, it was recreated to Miklós Ybl's design and moved to Erzsébet tér, leaving only this forlorn reminder to the former beauty of Kálvin tér.

The whole area around here has a depressing feel, but recovery is on hand down Üllői út in the shape of another of Ödön Lechner's playful buildings, the **Museum of Applied Arts** (Iparmüvészeti Múzeum) at No. 33-7. Built in 1896 as part of the Millennium celebrations, this was Lechner's first attempt at creating a Hungarian style of architecture and it was also the first attempt in Budapest to work with art nouveau forms. In some ways, the building is more of a clash of styles than a synthesis, and yet it manages to shine with brilliance. The facade is simple, although the colourful tiled roof still has some of the heaviness of eclecticism. The entrance hall, on the other hand, is a wild folk art fantasy, with red, blue and yellow tiles, a yellow and white floral ceiling, pale pink marble steps and Byzantine sand-coloured pillars. The interior shocks by its contrast: a modern steel-girdered ceiling captures light into the pure white wedding cake hall, textured with oriental zig-zags and art nouveau swirls and topped with an exquisite stained glass window. The museum itself is definitely the secondary attraction. The permanent folk craft exhibition is lacking in innovation (and English explanations), but the temporary exhibitions of furniture, tapestries and clothing are very well presented and utilize the space imaginatively. The nearby metro station, Ferenc körút, on the large ring-road, leads quickly back to the centre of town.

Right
The curvaceous oriental interior of the Museum of Applied Arts.

ANDRÁSSY ÚT AND HEROES' SQUARE

Pest blossomed in the forty years following the setting up of the Dual Monarchy in 1867. Hungarian national aspirations were running high, bringing unprecedented commercial and cultural development. In 1868, Prime Minister Gyula Andrássy returned from a trip to Paris with the idea of reorientating the map of Budapest around the city's new sense of importance by creating a grand boulevard running from the small ring-road, across the large ring-road and out to the park. In 1872, over two-hundred single storey houses were torn down to make way for the two-kilometer long **Andrássy út**. Within 15 years, the entire stretch was lined with elegant five-storey apartment blocks, department stores and villas.

The result is an axis of unparalleled unity, the homogeneity animated by the inherent diversity of the eclectic style. In 1896, the underground railway running the length of the street was completed, removing the danger that tram tracks would disrupt the harmony. For a few years, the boulevard was called simply Sugár út (Radial Avenue). But once it received Andrássy's name at his death in 1890, this stuck in the popular mind, despite the frequent official switches to Stalin Avenue in 1947, Avenue of Hungarian Youth for a few months in 1956, and then the unpronounceable Népköztársaság (People's Republic) from 1957-90. Count Andrássy, a great friend of Empress Elizabeth, was appointed prime minister in 1865, in the final run-up to the Compromise with Habsburg Austria. Five years later, Franz Joseph selected him to be the Austro-Hungarian foreign minister, sealing the link of near-equality between the dual poles of the Empire.

Appropriate to his political role, the first building on the left corner, a glorious example of the fusion of classical lines with romantic details from 1882, now bears a plaque commemorating the new era of friendship between the Austrians and Hungarians, ushered in by the cutting of the barbed-wire curtain in 1989. Across the road at No. 3, the **Postal Museum** provides an opportunity to delve behind the facades. The stairways of this residential block from 1886 are a dazzling display of frescoes, stained glass and wrought-iron detailing. The museum on the first floor occupies what used to be the spacious apartment of a certain Andreas Saxlehner who became wealthy selling medicinal water. The luxurious silk wall coverings, marble fireplace and ornate wooden detailing are still intact, and the exhibits — old telephone boxes, post office counters from the beginning of the century — are delightful.

Left
Vajdahunyad Castle in the City Park.

György Zala's Chariot of War.

The ornate courtyard of the Postal Museum.

A short way up on the left, we come to one of the gems of Andrássy út, the **Opera House**. Count Andrássy managed to persuade Franz Joseph to provide financial backing for the project, and the theatre was built from 1873-1884 by Miklós Ybl. Standing back from the street, the opera's exterior exudes a quiet classical graciousness. Inside, the modesty reaches only into the entrance hall, which had to be scaled down for lack of funds. The auditorium itself glitters in a gold and scarlet display of magnificence, complemented by a gilded marble foyer decorated with frescoes by Károly Lotz and Mór Thán, around which run intimate passages paneled with oak and draped in

blue and gold silk. The main marble stairway sweeps through the building, creating a breathtaking atmosphere of spatial harmony. The opera house is only open during performances (the box office is on the left side of the building). At the opening performance in 1884, held in the presence of Franz Joseph, the Hungarian composer Franz Liszt was prohibited from playing the piece he had written for the occasion; it contained a musical reference to the song of the Kurúts army which had fought the Habsburgs in the 17th century! The complementary neo-Renaissance building across the road from the opera is the **Drechsler House**, its ground-floor and arcade

Miklós Ybl's Opera House at night.

Page 75
*The gold and scarlet main
hall of the Opera House.*

formerly housing a famous coffee-house frequented by journalists. Astonishingly, this traditional structure from 1884, now occupied by the ballet school, was built by the young Ödön Lechner, a decade before he began to develop his unique Hungarian style. Andrássy út used to have a hectic cafe life. The building next to the opera, now the Goethe Institute, was once the Three Ravens Inn, a literary cafe, where the passionate early 20th century poet Endre Ady spent much of his time. Ady was closely associated with the influential journal, Nyugat (The West), forum of intellectuals from Ödön Lechner to Béla Bartók and Ady himself, who were interested in fusing Hungarian folk traditions with the progressive trends of Western culture. Decried as decadent cosmopolitans by the growing number of conservative nationalists, the journal increasingly came to represent one side of a conflict that pitted urban socially-aware and often Jewish cosmopolitans against largely anti-Semitic Magyar nationalists. With the collapse of the Habsburg Empire in 1918, the conflict burst out of the literary realm into two disastrous political extremes: the "red terror" of Béla Kun's short-lived Council Republic, followed by the "white terror" of Admiral Horthy's authoritarian regime. Ironically, both of these men were tutored in their youth by giants of modern culture: Béla Kun by Endre Ady, and Admiral Horthy by James Joyce at the Berlitz School in Trieste! Back across the road at No. 29 is one of the two remaining coffee-houses, the **Müvész (Artists) Cafe**. Shorn of the political tensions of earlier times, the back room has the feel of an old bourgeois salon fittingly furnished and populated. The coffee and cakes are beautifully served and very good.

A little further up, Andrássy út is intersected by the colourful **Nagymezö utca**. The section to the left is known with some exaggeration as Broadway, housing three theatres and the green-tiled shell of the former Arizona nightclub. To the right is the Ernst Museum at No.8; this has interesting exhibitions of modern art on the first floor, but it's worth going into the building just to look at the spectacular entrance hall and stairway, designed by Ödön Lechner in 1912, showing the influence on his later work of the more geometrical art deco style. The stained glass window was designed by József Rippl-Ronai. Across the street at No. 3 is a tall, thin red-brick newspaper building with a similar art deco touch. Back on Andrássy út, the **Divatcsarnok department store** at No. 39 represents one of the few divergences from the prevailing architectural style of the boulevard. Its bold parabolic arched window spanning the entire facade is a dash of art nouveau made possible in 1909 by a fire in the original casino building. The architect, Zsigmond Sziklai, erected an innovative multi-storey steel frame inside the building following the shape of the window. Sadly, the communist focus on the more mundane aspects of life has transformed this exciting interior into a sorry display of aesthetic and material deprivation, with patches of flowery wallpaper, screens obscuring the view to the exterior and a selection of goods that are unlikely ever to find buyers. But as a consolation at the very back of the store, between the first and second floors and not quite obscured by a railed door, is the resplendent 19th Lotz Hall, part of the

Right
*A seated statue of Franz
Liszt adorns the facade of
the Music Academy.*

Right
Art nouveau stairway in the Music Academy.

original casino. It's now used for Christmas sales.

At the next intersection stands a rather ugly socialist realist statue of Endre Ady. From here, Liszt Ferenc tér runs down to the right, past a lively rendering of the great Hungarian composer in full musical swing, to the **Music Academy** (Zeneakadémia) on the corner with Király utca. Built by Giergl and Korb in 1907, the academy's facade is a genial if rather heavy combination of eclecticism with art nouveau ornamentation, dominated by a large seated statue of Franz Liszt by Alajos Stróbl. The plans had originally incorporated Lecher's style of ornamentation, but in 1902 the Ministry of Culture refused to give state resources for this kind of architecture. The interior, however, is pure art nouveau, a dazzling blend of marble, tiles and frescoes. During the day, the side entrance on Király utca is open; after admiring the entrance hall, go up the colourful stairs and take a look into the concert hall from the gallery. The sober wooden panelling is brought to life with gold and silver detailing, carved swans, and a glorious triangular arrangement of organ pipes. Tickets for concerts here can be purchased at the Central Ticket Office at Vörösmarty tér 2.

One block up from Liszt tér, Andrássy út emerges at a major junction with the large ring-road. The square now bears its original and appropriate name, **Oktogon**, but for over forty years it was officially known as November 7 tér in commemoration of the Russian Revolution, intersecting with Lenin (now Teréz) körút; before that, the Oktogon spent a decade under Mussolini's name. In both of these violent eras, the building at No. 60 Andrássy út was a centre of terror. From 1939-45 it was the headquarters of the Hungarian Nazi party, the Arrow Cross; after the war, it was taken over by the Stalinist secret police until 1953. A new plaque on the wall commemorates the victims who were tortured here during these dark times.

The 1930s interior of the Lukács coffee-house.

In the more peaceful years of the 19th century, Franz Liszt established the first Budapest music academy across the road in the corner building (No. 67), with its entrance on Vörösmarty utca 35. Still part of the academy, and correspondingly resounding with music, the **Liszt Museum** occupies the first floor, in the rooms that were his apartment during his last years. The rich Biedermeier furnishings — gold and turquoise silk wall coverings, ornate pianos — make a wonderful setting for this tiny museum that documents (in English) the composer's life and work. Liszt was a German speaker with, as he put it, "a lamentable ignorance of the Hungarian language". But in his later life, he dedicated himself to developing the culture of Hungarian music. The grand neo-Renaissance building next to the museum used to be an exhibition hall but now houses the Puppet Theatre. Across the road at No. 70, the fusty facade hides one of the most beautiful coffee-houses in Budapest, the Lukács. Its lower room exudes the cool elegance of the 1930s, while the raised room has the voluptuous decor of a baroque palace. The cafe was expropriated from the Lukács family in 1949 and for several years given over to the secret police from down the road.

The Andrássy út opens out once again into the **Kodály körönd**, a fine circle of monumental rounded buildings, named after the composer

Neo-Renaissance facade of the Pallavicini Palace.

Zoltán Kodály, who worked with Béla Bartók collecting original folk music. In 1938, in line with the Horthy regime's new pro-German direction, it was renamed Adolf Hitler tér. A joke from those years tells how the underground stations now ran Mussolini Square, Hitler Square, Zoo, End Station — irony with more than a little truth. From here onwards, Andrássy út takes on a more spacious air, the classical urban blocks giving way to elegant villas surrounded by gardens. The splendid axis shooting up to the Millennium column of Heroes' Square is framed with ornate black street-lights. These signs of the old world reappeared recently, each one financed by a corporate sponsor commemorated on a small plaque. The ambience on this part of the boulevard makes for leisurely wandering, but there is still one building worth exploring. The **Pallavicini Palace** at No. 98 has a sleepy overgrown courtyard (to the left of the entrance) that is a copy of that in the Palazzo Marini in Milan.

The imposing triumphal colonnade and column at **Heroes' Square** (Hősök tere) was originally planned as part of the Millennium celebrations held in 1896 to commemorate 1000 years of Hungarian history since the "taking of the land" by Magyar tribes. The occasion was a glorification of the Dual Monarchy, and the

Millennium Monument was to reflect royal continuity and pride.
Building began once the celebrations were over and, in the face of
changing circumstances, dragged on for years. Albert Schickedanz
built the main structure and György Zala worked on the sculptures,
first creating the statue of the angel Gabriel, which has perched on
top of its column since 1910. According to Hungarian legend,
Gabriel appeared to Pope Sylvester II, urging him to recognise István
as a Christian king. The apostolic double cross and the Hungarian
crown represent the inseparable unity of the Hungarian kingdom and
the Christian West. Underneath the pillar are the fierce and exotic-
looking leaders of the seven Magyar tribes led by Árpád. The inner
pillars of the colonnade are topped with symbolic figures of startling
intensity and drama. On the left, the flailing figure of War whips his
horses into a frenzy; on the right, Peace calmly urges her horses
forward, proudly bearing a palm leaf in her hand.
Up to this point the monument was uncontroversial. The problems
began in selecting the 14 statues to grace the colonnades. In the
monument's original incarnation, more or less completed by 1914,
the five statues to the right were Habsburg monarchs. But the
collapse of the Austro-Hungarian Empire in 1918, following defeat in

*Italian courtyard in the
Pallavicini Palace.*

World War I, undermined the whole concept of the monument. During Béla Kun's revolutionary Council Republic, which lasted from March to August 1919, the five Habsburgs were taken down; Franz Joseph was smashed to pieces and the others were defaced with slogans, including ironically "Long live the Council Republic"! The Habsburgs made a comeback under Admiral Horthy. In 1920, the Treaty of Trianon had not only shorn Hungary of two-thirds of its territory, it had outlawed the future succession of a Habsburg to the throne. Hungary, although once again a monarchy, had no king, and support of the Habsburgs came to represent both a snub to the Allies and a determination never to give up the greater Hungary that the integrity of the empire had secured. Franz Joseph was recast, this time in coronation robes rather than uniform, and the Millennium colonnade was once again complete. In 1929, the government placed a monument to the fallen heroes of the 1914-1918 war in front of the Gabriel pillar, engraved with "To the thousand-year boundaries", and Heroes' Square was named.

Hungary's involvement in the defeat of 1945 was largely a result of courting Germany to get back the lost territory. The more or less democratic government that took over in 1945 turned their backs on this policy. The Habsburgs were once again taken away and the stable Hungarian kings of the distant past were joined by a series of non-royal heroes who had made their names fighting Habsburg rule. The original heroes' memorial disappeared along with the Habsburgs into the vault of ideologically unacceptable monuments. A simple heroes' monument was rebuilt in 1956 and the monument finally came to rest, except for the skateboarders and bikers who have discovered the potential for heroics offered by the smooth black and white paving.

The metal reliefs under the statues depict an event from the life of each monarch. St. István on the far left is being crowned in AD 1000, Béla IV (fifth along) surveys the devastation of the Tatar invasions in 1241; on the other side, János Hunyadi defeats the Turks in the Battle of Belgrade in 1456, while his son, Mátyás, is surrounded by his circle of humanist scholars. Gábor Bethlen, the fascinating Calvinist leader of Transylvania, is shown making an alliance with the Bohemian nobles against the Habsburgs during the Thirty Years' War. The final relief depicts Lajos Kossuth rousing the peasants to rebel in the 1848-9 revolution.

After wallowing in the ups and downs of a thousand and some years of Hungarian history, it is a pleasure to retreat into the classical pillars of the **Museum of Fine Arts** (Szépmüvészeti Múzeum). The collection is remarkably good. Some of the best pieces, including Rafael's Madonna and Rembrandt's Old Rabbi, along with the bulk of the Spanish collection, which now boasts several outstanding El Grecos and Goyas, were sold to the nation (under pressure) by the wealthy noble Esterházy family. Among the Italian collection, there is a remarkable Giorgione portrait, along with works by Bassano and Corregio. German and Flemish old masters are well represented by a wonderful Memling triptych, a spellbinding Dürer portrait and a characteristically bepeopled Bruegel painting. The 19th and 20th century collection is small but has some excellent French

Heroes' Square.

*The Chariot of War and
the Gabriel Column,
looking down Andrássy út.*

impressionist work. The ground floor has two of Rodin's passionate
sculptures, along with some of his more prosaic busts. In a separate
room at the back of the hall is the graphics collection which includes
work by da Vinci, Dürer, Cezanne and Manet.

The Állatkerti körút runs around the side of the museum to the left,
passing the famous Gundel restaurant (recently privatized and

renovated). On the left is the ornate gateway of the **Zoo** (Állatkert), incorporating elephants in its base, birds and plants in the mosaic arch, and a circle of polar bears around the dome. From a zoological perspective, the place has little to recommend it, but some of the buildings, erected in 1907-12, have an enchanting and playful art nouveau touch that is worth a quick look. The entrance was designed

The Magyar chieftains and the Chariot of War.

85

Playing chess in the hot pool at the Széchenyi Baths.

Page 86
El Greco - Study of a Man, circa 1590

Pieter Bruegel the Elder - St. John the Baptist Preaching, 1566

Page 87
Paul Cezanne - Buffet, circa 1873-77

Francisco de Goya - The Water-Seller, before 1812

by Kornel Neuschloss-Knüsli who was also responsible for the elephant house, an oriental fantasy in green tile. A ceramic elephant head protrudes from the doorway, while hippopotamuses and rhinoceroses emerge from the side domes. The Parisian Eiffel company built the iron and glass palm house, while the rustic wooden houses with long sloping roofs were designed by Károly Kos, who used Transylvanian folk architecture as the source of his work.
The elegantly voluptuous but fading golden yellow building across the road from the zoo is the **Széchenyi Baths** (Széchenyi Fürdő), one of the truly wonderful institutions of Budapest. Fed by a nearby artesian spring, the complex contains three sections. This entrance leads to two outdoor pools, one luke-warm the other hot, spaciously arranged inside the beautiful baroque walls. In winter especially, the pool is an amazing sight; the hot water produces a thick mist, in which sit groups of men playing chess on floating boards. To wallow in the water and run through the freezing air to the large tiled sauna is an experience unlike any other. Around the corner to the right at the side entrance is a mixed indoor thermal bath without the character of the other sections. The front of the building, an older

part built in grey stone, opens into a hallway as ornate as a concert hall, with old-fashioned signs in German and French pointing to the separate men's and women's steam and thermal baths. Here the foreign languages end and the over-sized naked bodies begin, moving from pool to pool, through steam and sauna, to get a final soap and water pummeling in the massage room.

Walk across the park towards the romantic **Vajdahunyad Castle**, actually an architectural folly comprising elements of over twenty different Hungarian buildings from the last thousand years. This lakeside castle was the centre-piece of the Millennium celebrations in 1896, designed by that most eclectic of architects, Ignác Alpár, whose statue now stands by the bridge proudly gazing at his creation. The original imitation was intended, like the other pavilions dotted around the City Park, to be pulled down once the year was over. But it turned out to be so popular that it was rebuilt in more permanent materials. Despite the slight air of Hollywood kitsch, the Romanesque-Gothic-Baroque complex is compelling, its enchanting fairy-tale towers furnishing a dramatic backdrop to the boaters in summer and the skaters in winter. In the evening, the floodlights pick out its rural contours, contrasting beautifully with the urban shadows thrown by the statues and colonnades on Heroes' Square. The medieval pinnacles that face the drawbridge are a scaled down copy of the Vajdahunyad Castle, János Hunyadi's Transylvanian home, built in 1450 and now in the Romanian town of Hunedora. Through the archway on the right is a medieval cathedral facade, copying several different churches, which then merges into a balcony in Italian Gothic style. On the right, a delightfully overgrown and peaceful Romanesque cloisters (Alpár's fantasy creation) merges into an intimate chapel, with an ornate portal. The voluptuous Baroque section is in the Austrian style of Fischer von Erlach, based on numerous noble palaces in the Hungarian countryside. This is the entrance to the rather dull **Museum of Agriculture** (Mezögazdasági Múzeum), with its mundane exploration of pig-farming and ploughing techniques. Nevertheless, it's worth going in to see the inside of the buildings. Up the grand chandeliered stairway, the round corner room has an interesting new exhibit of the drive to collectivism in the 1950s, complete with gaudy propaganda posters of determinedly happy socialist farm-workers and busts of Stalin. Back on the ground-floor, the passageway to the right of the entrance leads to the exotically painted Gothic rooms, dedicated to displays of hunting and fishing.

The hooded statue, opposite the entrance, represents **Anonymous**, the unknown medieval Hungarian chronicler who span wondrous and possibly true tales of the Árpád kings. He signed himself in Latin, "the notary of the great King Béla", but which of the four Bélas of the time no-one knows. Across the small bridge, a path runs around the lake passing the statue of George Washington, donated by the first wave of Hungarian-Americans. The path emerges back at Heroes' Square, outside the neo-Classical **Exhibition Hall** (Mücsarnok), the home of contemporary art. The metro station, diagonally across from the Hall, trundles back to the centre of town.

*The eclectic complex of
Vajdahunyad Castle.*

The Drinking Hall at the
Lukács Baths.

Plaques of gratitude on the
wall of the Lukács Baths.

RIVERSIDE BUDA

The Turks left few traces of their 145-year occupation of Budapest. With the victory of the armies of Christendom in 1686, their minarets were demolished and the mosques turned back into churches. Their culinary innovations, coffee and paprika, were soon absorbed into Hungarian culture, and Habsburg domination all but erased the memory of Turkish occupation. But not entirely. On the Buda river bank, concentrated around the Margaret Bridge (Margit Híd), shallow domed thermal baths, remnants of rose gardens, and street names still conjure up the spirit of the Turkish past.

To the right of Margaret Bridge, Frankel Leó út leads to the golden yellow Empire-style **Lukács baths**. The origins of this most 19th century looking institution reach back even beyond the Turks to the medieval Knights Hospitallers of St. John. But it was the Turks who introduced leisurely pleasure into what had been a strictly medicinal undertaking. In 1884, an entrepreneurial director built up a Grand Hotel around the old baths and turned the complex into an elegant international spa, catering to those with rheumatism. The cash-desk is inside a wonderfully decaying, marble-pillared kiosk, between the two gates, with "Ivócsarnok" (drinking hall) scrawled in 1950s neon on the outside. This building functions as the dispensing hall for the ill-smelling sulphurous medicinal water. The thermal baths, a 40° C pool with a pungent herbal steam room, are on the left of the courtyard, its wall covered with plaques of gratitude from ex-sufferers — written in everything from Arabic to Romanian and English. A door at the far end of the courtyard leads out to the front of the complex, yielding a glorious view of the grandeur and decrepitude of the building. Next to the Lukács baths and linked by modern buildings is the **Császár baths**, an even older institution. Past the small passageway to the left, amongst a jumble of modern structures, a set of tell-tale Turkish domes, pitted with tiny round windows, reveal the baths' origins. This part was built in 1571 on orders of the Pasha of Buda, Mustafa Sokoli, and was known as the Veli Beg. The narrow passageway between the two baths leads back on to Frankel Leó út. In a corner across the road, concealed by years of rust and neglect but still proudly topped by a spiked crescent, stands another **Turkish bath dome**, idly waiting for a (promised) revival. Next to it is a millpond where the springs bubble out of the earth; the Turks used it to drive a gunpowder mill. The houses in this street, beautiful if crumbling examples of early 19th century neo-Classicism, were built by József Hild, and were originally spa hotels

The Frankel Leó synagogue, enclosed inside a courtyard.

linked to the Császár baths. It's worth taking a short detour up the road to No. 49 to see one of the oddities of Jewish Budapest — a six-storey brick apartment building embracing an intimate neo-Gothic synagogue in its courtyard. The synagogue, built by Sándor Fellner in 1888, originally stood in a large park; the apartment block was added in 1928, and its facade decorated with a menorah (7-branched candelabra) and stars of David to provide a hint of what lies behind. Back towards the Margaret Bridge, the narrow cobbled **Gül Baba utca** runs steeply up hill to the right, a reminder of the colourful rambling streets that used to characterize Buda before the onset of 19th century concepts of progress and modernity. At the top, Mecset (Mosque) utca leads left to the **Gül Baba tomb**, now a Muslim shrine owned by the Turkish government. Gül Baba was a whirling dervish and a member of the bellicose Bektashi order. After a life of distinguished military service, he participated in the takeover of Buda Castle in 1541 but died the next day of a stroke in the middle of the thanksgiving service held in the rapidly transformed Mátyás Church. Pasha Mohammed ordered a grand burial for the dervish, and thus arose the octagonal domed building, surrounded by rose bushes, that looks very much like a Turkish bath. Since the name, Gül Baba, means "Father of the Roses", legends arose that he was responsible for planting the thousands of roses that used to adorn the Rose Hill (Rózsadomb) that rises up beyond the tomb. His early death make this unlikely; indeed the name may have more to do with the roses of blood that he delighted in creating with his sword. The roses of Rose Hill disappeared in later years to make way for vineyards; but these were hit by an attack of phylloxera, leaving the slopes to blossom with the villas of Budapest's rich and famous.

The tomb's terrace looks out over the river and offers an unusual view of Castle Hill, dominated not by the Palace or Mátyás Church but by the imposing edifice of the **State Archives**. From here we drop down the other side, following Margit utca to the main Mártírok utca, named after the martyrs killed in a military prison here during the "white terror" of Admiral Horthy's inter-war regime. Just before the bridge, turn right by the ferocious statue of a lion commemorating the Hungarian defence of the Przemysl fortress in southern Poland during the First World War. The street leads to Bem tér and the statue of **József Bem**, a famous Polish general who fought with the Hungarians in 1849. At the beginning of the 1956 revolution, a group of demonstrators marched here from the Petőfi statue in Pest to show their support for Polish attempts at reform. Bem himself never returned to Poland; he escaped to Turkey, converted to Islam, reorganized the Turkish army and became the Pasha of Aleppo, where he died in 1854.

Fő utca (High Street) runs the length of Watertown (Víziváros), a strange and chaotic mix of high grey 19th century apartment blocks and low colourful Rococo houses, interspersed with striking views up to the Castle. After years of severe flooding, a quay was built to control the Danube, raising the street level by over a meter to its present level. This explains why the pavement suddenly drops down to the entrances of the 18th century houses. The golden yellow Greek Catholic **Florian chapel** at No. 90, built in the 1700s, was

The narrow Gül Baba utca leads uphill to the dervish's tomb.

raised 140 centimeters in 1938 to compensate. In a glorious contrast of colours and styles, this Baroque church leads to the exotic collection of crescent-topped Turkish domes and the vivid green neo-Classical facade that make up the **Király baths**. These were built in 1570 by Pasha Sokoli Mustafa, the great patron of the bathing cult in Buda. This is probably the most atmospheric of all the thermal baths. Thin rays of light fall from the tiny windows that stud the dome, disappearing into the steaming thermal waters of the central pool. The three smaller domes cover the steam room, the showers and the chilly waters designed for post-steam dousing. The entrance to the baths is in the green extension, added in 1727, and decorated with round windows and a stone balcony.

The next block is dominated by the red-brick **Military Court of Justice**, built in 1915. From March 1944 to the end of December, the German Gestapo was stationed here, and used the building as a military prison. But contemporary Hungarians have a different association with the foreboding building; it was here that Imre Nagy, the Communist leader of the 1956 revolution, was held until his secret execution in June 1958. His rehabilitation and official funeral in June 1989 was one of the harbingers of the collapse of communist power. Two plaques have now joined the one commemorating the victims of Nazism on the back corner of the building; one to Nagy and one to the victims of communist terror. Following considerable

Gül Baba's octagonal tomb on Rose Hill.

public pressure, the square here was renamed Nagy Imre tér; the government was wary of glorifying the name of an avowed communist.

Past the Church of the Elizabeth Order on the left, the three-sided **Batthyány tér** opens spectacularly on to a view of the Parliament across the Danube. This was the market centre of the Watertown and, despite its function as a transport hub for Buda, its peacefully elegant Baroque and Rococo facades still evoke the mood of a former age. Below street level, Fő utca runs first into the lurid lilac walls of the **Hikisch House**, built in 1795 by the owner, an architect who worked on the Church across the square. Next door is a splendid Rococo building from 1776, the former "**White Cross Inn**", its old ballroom used for carnivals and theater performances dominating the main facade. The inn had many famous visitors. Emperor Joseph II is rumoured to have stayed here in the late 18th century, along with the notorious philanderer, Casanova de Seingalt, whose name is immortalised in the scrawling neon sign that points to the Casanova Piano Bar. The tall grey building next door is in Hungarian Zopf style, an architectural deviation from Rococo prevalent in the 1790s and marked by the undulating roof shape. Here the 18th century harmony is rudely interrupted by an iron and glass **market hall**, one of the five erected by Samu Pecz in the 1890s.

The curvaceous twin towers of the **Church of St. Anne** (Szent Anna

The dome and crescent of Gül Baba's tomb, a Muslim site of pilgrimage.

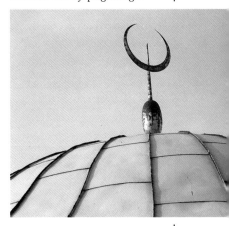

97

templom) are an unusual reminder of the influence of Italianate
Baroque that swept through Central Europe with the Jesuits, but left
little trace in Budapest. Built in 1740-46, the final touches were
added in 1805 by Kristóf Hikisch and the elliptical dome was
painted in the 1930s by Pál Molnar. During the dark years of the
early 1950s, **St. Anne's** was in danger of ideologically-inspired
demolition. Party leader, Mátyás Rákosi was extremely worried that
Stalin would visit him in his office in Parliament, look across the
river and be outraged at the all too visible remnants of religiosity.
Plans were drawn up to remove the church, ostensibly for the sake of
building the Batthyány tér metro, but Stalin's death in 1953 neatly
solved the problem. The former presbytery next door houses the
Watertown's best cafe, the Angelika, one of the first private
businesses in Hungary with a correspondingly comfortable interior
and friendly service.

Fő utca continues past the red-brick multitude of towers and spires
that make up the **Calvinist Church**, built by Samu Pecz (of the
market halls) in 1896. Directly across, stands a handsome art
nouveau apartment block built in 1911, and Béla Bartók's home from
1922-8. At Corvin tér, the mish-mash of styles that characterises Fő
utca is at its most confused. The large eclectic building at the side is
the **Buda Vigadó**, a concert hall built in 1900 on the site of an old
arsenal; around the back are three delightful but decrepit Baroque
houses, framed by elegant balustrades leading up the hill.

Turning left on Halász utca, we come to the tree-lined pavement
along the banks of the Danube. The view here is spectacular: the
Parliament, Gresham Palace, St. Steven's and the Chain Bridge
unfold along the shore, topped on the Buda side by the dramatic
liberation monument of Gellért Hill. This is where we are headed.
The 10-15 minute walk along the river is stunning, interspersed with
ever-changing views of Pest and the Royal Palace, but the weary can

*The shallow green domes of
the Király Baths.*

*Left
The vivid green facade of
the Király Baths entrance
hall.*

*The twin Baroque towers
of St. Anne's Church on
Batthyány tér.*

99

take tram 19 two stops to Ybl Miklós tér. At this square, the ornate series of steps and ramps of the **Castle Bazaar** lead up to the (now closed) castle gardens, looking, according to a report from 1896, "like a fairy apparition rising out of the waves of the Danube". The dilapidated reality is less magical; steel braces now hold the delicate balustrades in place and gates barr the curious visitor.

Aprod utca turns uphill to the right into the traffic-ridden remains of **Tabán**, one area of Buda that blossomed under the Turks, largely because of the two thermal baths here, the Rudas and the Rácz, both still in existence. The Turks called the district Debaghane, meaning tanners' quarter. The name was adapted to Tabanan by the Serbian settlers who came here during the 18th century. In the 19th century, Tabán was populated by Serbs, Greeks and gypsies, most of whom made their living from the river, but this was also the home of the brothels and gambling dens. Most of the rambling old houses were

Looking over the roofs of the Watertown to the Chain Bridge.

Left
The facade of St. Anne's Church.

101

Left
Statues and dome on the
Castle Bazaar.

cleared away in the early years of this century because of the constant
outbreak of epidemics, and others were destroyed during the war. All
that is left of old Tabán is the early 18th century **Aranyszarvas**
(Golden Stag) restaurant to the right, and the golden yellow **Church of
St. Christine's** (1736) and **Semmelweiss house** (1790) on the left.
Tabán Park on the other side of the network of main roads has
recently acquired a new attraction, two thin graffiti-covered sections
of the **Berlin Wall**, gradually being chipped away by night-time
souvenir collectors. Standing alone by the roadside, the pieces of wall
could easily be mistaken for the vandalized remnants of some
socialist playground; but maybe that is the intention. Further back in
the park is the modest golden yellow facade of the Rácz (Serbian)
baths, fed by a thermal spring that was already in use in the 14th
century. The old baths was rebuilt by Miklós Ybl in 1870, who gave
it its characteristic eight-cornered dome.

Tabán with the Golden
Stag Inn, the Semmelweiss
House and St. Catherine's
Church.

Looking out over the Danube with St. Gellért.

Rising above the Rácz baths is the steep dolomitic cliff-face of **Gellért Hill**. This strange rocky outcrop was formed by a geological fault which is also the origin of the numerous springs in this area. The path up is less steep than it looks, reaching the enormous statue of St. Gellért in 10-15 minutes, and the Citadella in a further 15-20 minutes. It is also possible to take a bus (No. 27 from Moricz Zsigmond tér) or a taxi up to the top. But the path yields unusual views of the Palace and Pest which it would be a shame to miss. At the first viewing point (a small wooden bridge), the shallow tortoise-shell Turkish dome of the Rudas Baths on the bank of the river is in clear view. Behind it runs the sleek modern lines of the Elizabeth bridge, the only one to have been completely remodelled after the destruction of 1945.

The enormous **statue of St. Gellért** defiantly raising a cross (Gyula Jankovics, 1904) is best appreciated at night from the Elizabeth bridge. But despite the rather shabby state of the monument up close, there is something very grand about standing within the semicircle of stone columns and looking out with Bishop Gellért. It was from this spot that pagan rebels were supposed to have rolled the Italian missionary in a spiked barrel down the cliff into the Danube in 1046. The statue was one of ten donated to Budapest in 1897 by Franz Joseph, who was perturbed — difficult as it is to imagine now — by the absence of monuments.

The top of the hill is dominated by the flat, mean-looking **Citadella**. The Habsburgs built the fortress with forced labour after putting down the 1848-9 revolution. It was completed in 1854, but by this time tensions were already beginning to abate. With the successful conclusion of the 1867 Compromise, the Hungarians exerted considerable pressure to have the hated fortress demolished. Architects came up with grandiose plans for parks, memorials and waterfalls, but once it was turned over to the city in 1897, the council decided that demolition would be too expensive. In a show of symbolic nationalism, one wall was partially dismantled. The citadel still exudes an uncomfortable feel, but it's worth going inside for the excellent view it provides over Budapest. Having failed to rid the hill of one remnant of foreign occupation, it was soon saddled with another. In 1947 the Soviet **liberation monument** was erected here. Ironically, the somewhat grotesque statue of a wind-swept women holding aloft a palm-leaf of peace was originally commissioned from Zsigmond Kisfaludi Stróbl as a memorial to Admiral Horthy's pilot son killed during the war. Political circumstances shifted and a few moderations were required to adapt the statue into a monument to Soviet liberation: the sculptor removed the wings turning the angel into a woman and switched the planned propeller into a palm leaf, and the Soviets were happy. In 1992, after months of debate on how to deal with the monument, the red soldier standing below the main statue was symbolically removed leaving the rest of the statue intact, if a little bare.

The Liberation Monument.

From here it is a 10 minute walk down to the **Gellért Hotel and Baths**, a vast white-domed pleasure palace of a building. Built in 1911-18 by Artúr Sebestyén and Ármin Hegedűs, the complex is a wonderful example of late art nouveau. The impressive arched side entrance leads into the Thermal Baths (Gyógyfürdő), comprising separate thermal pools and steam baths for men and women, a wonderfully ornate mixed swimming pool and an outdoor pool in summer. The baths, unlike the hotel next door, have retained their original art nouveau decor, with intricate mosaics, stained glass windows and sensuous statues. Of all the baths in Budapest, these are the easiest for a foreigner to manoeuvre around in, but the more modern, cosmopolitan atmosphere makes for a less exotic feel than in the old Turkish baths.

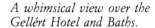

A whimsical view over the Gellért Hotel and Baths.

A short way along the river bank from the Gellért Hotel is a mysterious black monastery and **grotto church**, built into the cliffs. This was erected in 1932 by the Paulines, who had lost their church in Pest when Joseph II dissolved their order in 1786. The communists put a stop to their brief comeback and the sacred complex was given over to the ballet school which used it as a hostel. The little chapel has recently been reconsecrated and the building is now being renovated, ready for the resurgent Paulines to try once again.

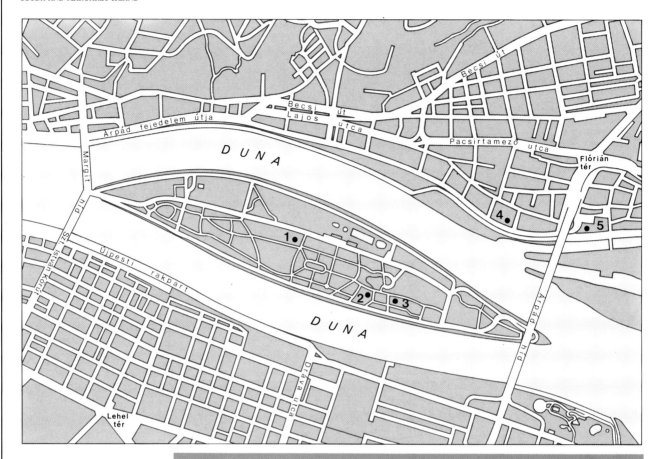

1. *Ruins of Franciscan
   monastery*
2. *Ruins of Dominican
   monastery*
3. *St. Michael's Chapel*
4. *Former synagogue*
5. *Zichy Palace*

*Óbuda's main square, with
the turn-of-the-century town
hall.*

Page 106
View of Pest from the Gellért Hill.

Page 107
The art nouveau splendour of the Gellért Hotel and Baths.

ÓBUDA AND MARGARET ISLAND

The history of Budapest began in **Óbuda** (Ancient Buda). In 15-11 BC, Romans conquered the Western part of Hungary, creating the province of Pannonia. A Roman legion camp was established in the heart of today's Óbuda, and a civilian town, Acquincum, grew up a little further north. In 106 AD, Emperor Trajan made the now bustling town of Acquincum the capital of Lower Pannonia. During the 1st and 2nd centuries, Acquincum flourished. But in the 3rd century, the military town burned down, and by 350 AD roving tribes had virtually destroyed Acquincum. In 409 AD, the Huns took over the Danube, their leader Attila ruling over the ruins of the Roman camp. After the Huns came a series of Germanic tribes — the Ostrogoths, Gepids, Longobards and the Avars — all settling for a while around Acquincum. Until finally, in 896 or thereabouts, the Magyar tribes emerged from the mists of history and brought Christianity and civilisation to the land. The Árpád kings lived in Óbuda until the devastating Tatar invasions of 1240-1 persuaded them to move to the more easily defensible Castle Hill. In the early 1300s, religious orders moved into Óbuda bringing new life to the town and the old castle became the queen's residence. Its medieval grandeur was destroyed during the Turkish occupation. But in the 1700s, the wealthy Zichy family gradually transformed the ruins into a busy but elegant oasis of Baroque churches and palaces.

Baroque fantasy on the Zichy Palace.

Unfortunately, today's Óbuda does not live up to its rich history. After waves of invasion and occupation, followed by rebuilding, the final onslaught came in the 1960s in the shape of socialist housing policies. The old streets and squares were razed and replaced by the vast bridgehead of the Árpád Bridge and block after block of anonymous flats. Still, scattered in between the ugliness, there are incongruous remnants of outstanding beauty — a row of Roman pillars, a richly coloured Baroque palace, a classical temple-like synagogue — bravely defying the arrogance of modernity.

The best place to start exploring Óbuda is the base of the Árpád Bridge, easily reached by the local HÉV train from Batthyány tér (stop: Árpad Híd). The large white building at Szentlélek tér 1 is part of the **Zichy palace** complex built in the 1750s and now houses the **Vasarely Museum**. Victor Vasarely, the Hungarian-born French artist who became famous in the 1960s for his dynamic and colourful geometrical paintings, donated almost 400 of his works to this specially designed museum. In addition to numerous examples of the geometric genre, the collection shows the development of his work from textile designs and abstract but still recognizable subjects.

Imre Várga's "Strollers in the Rain".

Around the corner in the same complex, a gateway leads into a charmingly neglected courtyard, facing the delicate pink and white Rococo palace of Miklós Zichy. The ornate stone balcony, resting lightly on four pillars, was the creation of Zichy's favourite sculptor, Károly Bébo; who was also responsible for the statues that now stand forlorn and damaged but still powerful in the back of the garden. A second avantgarde collection is housed here, the **Kassak Museum**. Lajos Kassak was a constructivist, active during the 1920s and 1930s. After a period of disfavour during the 1950s, the communist government resurrected him as "the representant (sic) of the rise and the spiritual energy of the working class". Despite this inauspicious introduction, some of his work is fascinating and is complemented by temporary exhibitions of other artists influenced by cubism and dadaism.

Leaving this avant-garde world, we emerge into **Fő tér**, the showpiece of 18th century Óbuda, left untouched by the crusading zeal of the 1960s' planners. In Roman times, this square formed part of the military camp, and during the 17th century rebuilding it was once again the centre of Óbuda. The large town hall was built in 1903; its two ancient Hungarian caryatids (one with Attila-like plaits and a moustache) are typical of the more superficial attempts of the time to create a Hungarian style. To the right of the square, the

Mosaic Roman floor at the Herkules Villa.

main attraction of the winding Laktanya utca is signalled by the amusing group of statues, "**Strollers in the Rain**" by Imre Várga. His **museum** is in the low golden yellow house at No. 7. Várga, born in 1927 and still very active today, is a naturalistic sculptor whose statues are dotted not only throughout Budapest but also all around Europe. The museum is bursting with his works, which largely draw their inspiration from Hungarian themes. The centre-piece is a haggard but wise-looking St. István gazing at a golden Madonna; others deal with the tragedy of war and political conflict, always in a very personalised humanistic style.

Back at Főtér, the Hidfő utca leads straight into the heart of Óbuda's ugliness. Walking to the right along the mammoth split ceiling of the bridge road, steps lead into the underground labyrinth of **Flórían tér**. Hard as it is to imagine, this was the site of the Árpád Castle in the 12th century. Previously, it had been a major part of the Roman military camp. Immediately on the right is the **Roman Baths Museum**, showing the substantial remains of the huge baths complex, built here in the late 1st century with shell-shaped pools and heated floors. Further on, the alienating orange passageways, scarred by vandalism, are filled with remnants of Roman Óbuda. An opening to the right reveals a stately row of Roman pillars incongruously juxtaposed against a vast concrete block.

111

Undulating tiled roofs on Dugovics utca, with the Church of St. Peter and Paul in the background.

Óbuda's neo-Clàssical synagogue, now a TV studio.

Those who want to see more Roman remains can cross back under the road and walk up Vihar utca for five minutes to see the intricate mosaic floors of the **Herkules Villa** (from around 200 AD), situated on the right at Meggyfa utca 19-21.

Back in Flórían tér, the passageway leads out to the other side of the bridge road, past large prints on the walls revealing Budapest's appearance throughout the centuries, with a particularly fascinating one from 1684 showing a Habsburg attack on the minaret-spiked city skyline. As we emerge, Kálvin köz runs to the right. On the corner we are greeted by an intimately rural vicarage, built in 1909 by Károly Kos who spearheaded the development away from art nouveau to a progressive folk-based architecture. To the left, skirting around one of the new blocks, **Dugovics utca** reveals another row of low 18th century houses, with spectacularly undulating tiled roofs. This area has the feel of a wasteland, salvaged by these patches of humanity. Further ahead, the inviting golden yellow **Church of St. Peter and Paul** brings us to the post-modern reflecting glass Acquincum Hotel, as out of place as any of the other buildings here. Concealed behind the huge bulk of the hotel is yet another incongruous facade; an elegant pale yellow neo-Classical temple, formerly the main **Óbuda synagogue** and now a TV studio. When Maria Theresa banned Jews from living in Buda in 1746, they moved

Autumn on Margaret Island.

Stepping stones on Margaret Island.

113

St. Michael's Chapel on Margaret Island.

to this area of Óbuda, under the protection of the aristocratic Zichy family. At this time, Jews made up over 40% of the population, living in the tiny ghetto houses that used to clutter this area. The synagogue was built in 1769, but given its present appearance, complete with six Corinthian columns, in 1821 by Andreas Landherr. Árpád Bridge spans the Danube at the top end of **Margaret Island** (Margitsziget), accessible at this point by taxi and on foot. The island functions as a vast park, laid out in the 1790s by Palatine Joseph. Until the Second World War, this was the playground of the rich and elegant; lower classes were neatly excluded by the entrance fee. The old Grand Hotel, built by Miklós Ybl, still reflects the tranquil grandeur of this age, but its new neighbour, the Thermal Hotel, bears witness to the less exclusive nature of the island today. Beyond the hotels, a wooded area dotted with statues of Hungary's writers and composers, encloses the remains of two of the religious orders that settled here in the 13th century. The tiny neo-Romanesque **St. Michael's Chapel** was rebuilt in the 1930s on the site of a Premonstratensian monastery and boasts a 15th century bell that was only rediscovered in 1914 after a storm uprooted a tree. The medieval stone ruins further down are all that is left of the **Dominican monastery**, built by Béla IV in the mid-13th century.

The Water Tower.

Having escaped to Dalmatia during the devastating Tatar invasions of 1240, Béla had vowed to dedicate his daughter to God if he would deliver Hungary from the brutal scourge. His prayers were answered: the Tatars disappeared as quickly as they had come, scurrying back to Karakorum in 1241 to fight over the succession to the Mongol throne. The convent was built on what was then called Hare Island, the royal hunting ground; nine-year old Margaret was duly delivered to its doors, where she became a fanatical nun until her death at the age of 28, and the island was renamed after her. In 1943, she was sainted and a gravestone, always covered in flowers, erected among the ruins. Lower down, the ruins of yet another monastery, belonging to the Franciscans jostle with those of the Palatine's villa. During the Turkish occupation, the monasteries were destroyed and the holy ground taken over by the Pasha's harem! Behind the conspicuous and shapely **water tower**, built in 1911 by Rezsö Ray, is a large open-air theatre. On the Western shore between the Franciscan and Dominican ruins is the enormous open-air Palatine swimming baths, with large pools of both warm and cool water. Past a charming animal farm, filled with peacocks, pheasants, deer and goats, the feather-shaped island tapers down to the Margaret Bridge.

ERZSÉBETVÁROS: THE JEWISH DISTRICT

Pest never had a Jewish ghetto in the traditional sense. Indeed, the emergence of the Jewish community in Pest, concentrated in Erzsébetváros, between Károly körút and Erzsébet körút, occurred during an era of gradual emancipation and growing strength. Until 1746, most Jews had lived in Buda; after being ousted by Maria Theresa, they went to Óbuda where they lived under aristocratic protection, making up over 40% of the population there in 1840. Pest opened its doors to Jews in 1800. Ironically given later developments, the emergence of nationalistic sensibilities in Hungary initially boosted the Jewish community's prestige. By the middle of the 19th century, most Jews were speaking Hungarian (rather than German) and had become enthusiastic Magyars. In 1840, Jews were allowed to buy property in towns for the first time. After the 1848-9 revolution, the Hungarian diet brought up the issue of full legal emancipation for Jews in recognition of their role in the national struggle, and this finally became a reality in 1867. Jews began to play an important role in the dynamic cultural and commercial growth of Pest, making up around 20% of the population by 1900.

The huge onion-towered **Dohány Synagogue**, located between Dohány utca and Wesselényi utca, was very much a product of this time. The fledgling community had leased the building site and the houses on Síp utca in 1837, and finalized the purchase in 1844. The architectural competition produced a selection of neo-Classical and Byzantine designs, but the community decided to commission the Viennese architect, Ludwig Förster, to realise his Moorish conception. Frigyes Feszl, famous for his Vigadó concert hall, also worked on the building. The synagogue was completed in 1859, a monumental structure seating 3,000, enlivened by the patterning of light and dark brick and given an Eastern flavour with the two copper cupolas. When cracks began to appear in the ceiling, Adam Clark who had become famous with his work on Chain Bridge was called in to carry out repairs.

At that time, the building was still joined to houses on one side, and it was in one of these that Theodor Herzl, the founder of the political Zionist movement was born in 1860. A bright new plaque commemorates the event. The houses were cleared in 1929 to build the square, domed **Heroes' Synagogue** (Hősök temploma) and the arcaded courtyard, linked harmoniously with the main synagogue by a building that now houses the **Jewish Museum** (Zsído Múzeum), open May-October. These two buildings are now undergoing extensive renovation, financed by the Emmanuel Fund, a trust set up by Tony

Left
The Moorish towers of the main Dohány synagogue.

The arcade of the Heroes's Synagogue.

Curtis (who is of Hungarian-Jewish origin) in 1987.
The courtyard, now called **Heroes' Cemetery** (Hősök temetöje)
became a mass grave for the thousands of Jews who were killed or
died of starvation in this area in 1944-5. Since the German
occupation of Hungary on March 19, 1944, Jews had been forced to
live in specially-designated "yellow-star" houses, awaiting Adolf
Eichmann's deportation orders. On October 15, the mildly anti-
Semitic Admiral Horthy was replaced in a German-backed coup by
Ferenc Szálasi, head of the notoriously brutal Arrow Cross party.
Immediately gangs of Arrow Cross thugs rampaged through the city,
killing hundreds of Jews, thousands were rounded up ready for
deportation, and the remainder (around 200,000) were relocated and
thrown into a closed ghetto in this area, enclosed by the two ring-
roads and between Király utca and Dohány utca. The ghetto was
surrounded by a wooden fence, built at the community's own
expense, with four gates at each side. Jews were allowed out of their
houses for two hours in the morning and two in the afternoon.
Leaving the ghetto meant almost certain death; as it was, gangs of
Arrow Cross would rush through the ghetto, killing indiscriminately
or taking victims to the Danube to be shot and thrown into the
water. Over 2,000 Jews were buried in a mass grave in the
courtyard; around 17,000 Jews were killed altogether during the short
duration of the ghetto which was liberated by the Soviet army on

*The new Memorial to the
Swiss emissary, Carl Lutz.*

*Right
Imre Várga's weeping
willow holocaust memorial.*

January 17, 1945. The silver **weeping willow monument**, designed by Imre Várga, was erected in 1987 in memory of the 600,000 Hungarian Jews killed during this time. The inscription in Hebrew reads, "Your pain is greater than my pain". One of the monuments in the cemetery records the heroic death of Hanna Szenes, a young Hungarian Jew living in Palestine who parachuted into Hungary in 1944 on a rescue mission; she was captured, tortured and finally executed, leaving only her remarkable poetry behind. The building next to the willow — its entrance is around the corner at Síp utca 12 — is the centre of the Jewish community. It was here, during the German occupation, that the Jewish council was forced to implement and finance Adolf Eichmann's orders, including requisitions, the wearing of the yellow star, ghettoization and deportations.

Walk up Wesselényi utca, turning left on Kazinczy utca. In the second half of the 19th century, wealthy Jews lived in the newly emerging prestige areas of Budapest around the parliament and along Andrássy út. Some even received noble titles in recognition of their contributions to Hungarian life. But the mass of poor Jews, many of them immigrants from the eastern provinces of the Empire, occupied the ghetto-like streets of this area, in some making up 70% of the population. A good portion of the 80,000 Jews now in Budapest — again the poorer ones — still live in this area. And the dank narrow streets, crumbling facades and intimate courtyards retain something of the claustrophobic atmosphere of those times. In the middle of the street is the orthodox **Kazinczy synagogue**, built in 1913 by Béla and Sándor Löffler. Its recessed position was designed to show off the majestic art nouveau facade. Now it serves only to emphasise the extent of its collapse: broken windows held in place by twisted lead panes, glorious flower-patterned but now rusting iron gates, and a dark covering of grime. The synagogue, remarkably, is still in use, and numerous unsettled plans are afoot to renovate the building. Around the corner at Dob utca 35, is the centre of the orthodox community, its school and the lively kosher restaurant, Hanna, backing on to the Kazinczy synagogue.

Throughout the Jewish quarter, inconspicuous entrances open on to fascinating courtyards, some with a rural feel, others bristling with wrought iron walkways. But at Dob utca 16, behind a set of wonderful art nouveau gates, there is a speciality even for this area. The **Gozsdu udvar** is a long passageway running through a series of apartment buildings to Király utca, forming one inner courtyard after another. A little further down on Dob utca, the eye is arrested by the formless red-brick facade of a transformer building, insensitively placed here in 1960. In 1991 the city council erected a very strange **memorial** at this bleak modern corner — a golden angel protruding from the wall holds a flowing robe that falls down to the ground where a bandaged man lies begging for help. This commemorates the activities of the Swiss emissary Carl Lutz who, along with the Swede, Raoul Wallenberg, risked his life to issue protective passes to Jews threatened by the German occupation. The plaque recites the Talmudic quotation, "Whoever saves even a single person, saves the whole world."

Wallenberg, who was picked up by the Soviets immediately after the

liberation and disappeared in mysterious circumstances in the Soviet Union, is commemorated in what is now called Raoul Wallenberg utca. This was the heart of the "international ghetto" also set up by Eichmann in October 1944, in the area behind the Szt. István körút, for holders of protective passes. The communist regime avoided setting up memorials to these men in deference to the Soviet Union's refusal to disclose information about the fate of Wallenberg. A second monument to Wallenberg, donated by the US ambassador and designed by Imre Várga, was finally erected in 1987 (in Buda on Szilágyi Erzsébet fasor, beyond the Hotel Budapest); the original statue built immediately after the war disappeared before its dedication without a trace.

The Raoul Wallenberg monument in Buda.

Rumbach utca, running off to the right, is the home of the first **orthodox synagogue** in Budapest, built in 1872 after the split between the reform and the orthodox tendencies. Its startling yellow Byzantine facade, topped with two white minaret-like towers, is one of the early works of Otto Wagner, who later became famous in Vienna for his innovative art nouveau (Jugendstil) buildings. The synagogue is built around an octagonal ground-plan, covered with a dome. Like the Dohány synagogue, the building is currently being renovated. The truncated Madach utca with its glorious arched red-brick apartment building runs back down to Károly körút into the central junction of Deák tér. Plans to extend Madach utca into a long boulevard were frustrated by the lowly courtyards of the Gozsdu udvar.

Otto Wagner's yellow and orange Rumbach synagogue.

There is an aesthetic tension in Budapest that matches the country's stormy political history. Repeatedly engulfed by invaders from both the West and the East, the city has absorbed elements of both while striving to find its own way. To the outsider, the result is fascinating — a mosaic of Central European influences from Habsburg to Turkish, French to Slavic, sometimes clashing discordantly, at other times fusing in a flash of unique brilliance that is peculiarly Budapest.

CHRONOLOGY

896   Magyar tribes under the leadership of Arpad move west from the Volga.

956   Magyars are defeated at the Battle of Lechfeld, then pushed out of western Europe and contained in the Danube Basin.

1001 Ist007E3n crowned "apostolic king" of Hungary by Pope Silvester II.

1222 King András II issues the Golden Bull guaranteeing constitutional rights to the nobles.

1241 Tatar invasions lay waste to Hungary, destroying the fledgling cities of Buda and Pest.

1244 King Béla IV builds Buda castle, bringing in German, Italian and Jewish settlers to repopulate the city; minorities rights to culture and language are guaranteed by a new Golden Bull.

1276 King Laszlo IV extends the castle and grants Buda Royal Free Town status.

1301 The Árpád dynasty dies out; struggle over succession ensues.

1308 Charles Robert of Anjou is crowned King of Hungary.

1342 King Lajos the Great expands the Hungarian empire into the Balkans and Poland (for a while) and stabilizes the economy by introducing the golden forint.

1387 Sigismund becomes the King of Hungary (later also King of Bohemia and Holy Roman Emperor); builds up Buda Castle and a string of fortresses against Turkish threat.

1456 János Hunyadi defeats the Turks at Belgrade, temporarily halting their advance against Christendom.

1458 Hunyadi's son, Mátytás Corvinus, is elected king of Hungary. The Royal Court becomes the centre of Renaissance culture, learning and architecture.

1470 Pest becomes a Royal Free Town with defensive town walls.

1490 Uláyszló Jagello II, King of Bohemia and Poland, becomes King of Hungary, moving the royal residence to Buda, under the agreement that the Habsburgs would assume the throne if he were to have no heir.

1514 A peasant rebellion under the leadership of György Doszsa is brutally put down, leading to the introduction of serfdom and numerous privileges for the nobility.

1526 Suleiman the Magnificent defeats the Hungarians at the Battle of Mohacs, at which Lajos II is killed putting an end to the Jagello dynasty. Turks begin to move in to Hungary.

1541 The Turks take over Buda Castle which becomes the seat of the Pasha.

1568 Hungary is formally divided into three parts by the Treaty of Adrianopole: Royal Hungary in the West under the Habsburg Emperor Ferdinand I, Turkish Hungary and Transylvania under the Turkish-supported noble John Zapolya.

1686 Habsburgs recapture Buda and Pest from the Turks and then take over the whole country including Transylvania.

1687 The Hungarian crown is declared to be hereditary in the House of Habsburg; Joseph is crowned King in Pozsony (Bratislava), still the Hungarian capital.

1703 Buda and Pest are restored to Royal Free Town status.

1712 Charles IV crowned king of Hungary in Pozsony; Habsburg power is consolidated.

1749 Maria Theresa begins to rebuild Buda castle.

1777 The University is moved from Nagyszombat (now Trnava, Czechoslovakia) to Buda.

1784 Joseph II moves the Royal Cabinet and military command to Buda from Pozsony, and moves the University to Pest.

1790 Pest begins to expand rapidly becoming the center of arts and learning; the walls are razed and the town soon has a larger population than Buda.

1838 The Great Flood destroys two-thirds of Pest; wide-scale construction programmes are introduced.

1839 Construction starts on the Chain Bridge, the first permanent link between Buda and Pest.

1848 Revolution breaks out against Habsburg rule at the instigation of Lajos Kossuth and Sándor Petöfi. The revolutionaries take over Buda Castle and establish their own government.

1849 The Habsburgs squash the revolutionaries with the help of the Czarist Russian army. Hungary loses Transylvania and Croatia, and becomes a Habsburg crownland, tightly controlled from Vienna.

1850 The Habsburgs build the Citadella on the top of Gellért Hill as a defence against future rebellion.

1867 Ferenc Deak negotiates the "Compromise" with the Habsburgs, who were weakened by their defeat at the hands of the Prussians; the Dual Austro-Hungarian Monarchy comes into being, giving the Hungarians considerable autonomy and restoring control over Transylvania and Croatia. Jews are given full legal equality. Franz Joseph and Elizabeth are crowned King and Queen of Hungary.

1872 The three towns, Buda, Pest and Óbuda, are united as Budapest.

1896 The Millennium celebrations, commemorating one thousand years since the Magyar tribes came to Hungary, is held in Budapest. The first subway line is opened.

1916 Karl and Zita are crowned King and Queen of Hungary.

1918 Count Mihaly Károly proclaims the independent Republic of Hungary, as Croatia, Transylvania and Upper Hungary (Slovakia) begin to break away from Hungary.

1919 Béla Kun, a supporter of the Soviet Revolution, proclaims the Hungarian Council Republic, which lasts for 133 days. Romanians invade the country and are turned back by Admiral Miklós Horthy.

1920 Horthy establishes an authoritarian government under the title of Royal Regent. A period of "white terror" leaves thousands dead. The Allies push through the

Treaty of Trianon, depriving Hungary of two-thirds of its former territory which goes to Romania, Yugoslavia, Czechoslovakia and Austria. An Anti-Jewish Law sets a quota on Jews in universities.

1927 Hungary forms an alliance with Mussolini's Italy.

1933 Hungarian Nazis form the Arrow Cross Party.

1938 Anti-Jewish Law sets a quota on Jews in the professions. Germany returns part of Slovakia to Hungary under the Munich Pact.

1939 Anti-Jewish law bans Jews from top positions. Germany returns Carpatho-Ruthenia to Hungary.

1941 Parts of Transylvania and Yugoslavia are returned to Hungary. Further anti-Jewish legislation is passed. Hungary enters into the war as an ally of Nazi Germany.

1944 Germany occupies Hungary on March 19. Adolf Eichmann starts Jewish deportations, Horthy prevents deportations from Budapest. After Horthy tries to get out of the war, the Germans establish a puppet regime under the Arrow Cross leader, Ferenc Szalási. Allied bombing of the city begins.

1945 The Soviet army liberates Pest in January and Buda in February. The pre-war Trianon borders are reinstated.

1946 The Hungarian Republic is proclaimed with a coalition government.

1948 The Communists, backed by the Red Army, take power following rigged elections and the absorption of the Social Democrats.

1949 Hungary becomes a People's Republic under dictator Matyas Rákosi. Numerous leading Communists and opposition figures are executed.

1953 Following Stalin's death, Moscow pushes Rákosi to appoint the reformist Imre Nagy as prime minister; Rákosi regains effective power after a period of tolerance.

1956 Rákosi is removed by Khrushchev; show trial victims are rehabilitated. Revolution breaks out, supported by Imre Nagy, in October; Communist symbols are destroyed, new parties formed, political prisoners released. The Soviet army invades in November and suppresses the revolution, killing 3,000 people. 200,000 Hungarians flee the country. János Kádár becomes Party leader.

1958 Imre Nagy is executed as a counter-revolutionary and buried in an unmarked plot with the other victims of 1956.

1968 Kádár introduces market-oriented "goulash communism"; but sends troops to Czechoslovakia to help quell the Prague Spring.

1979 Economic stagnation starts.

1988 Kádár abdicates in favour of reformist, Miklós Németh, who introduces political and economic reforms.

1989 Imre Nagy is rehabilitated at an official funeral. The Party is dissolved, and Hungary decides to cut the "iron curtain" border with Austria, to let out thousands of East Germans.

1990 Free elections lead to the defeat of the communists; a centre-right coalition government is formed.

RESTAURANT LIST

Budapest's restaurant scene has improved drastically over the last few years, but prices are beginning to approach Western levels. Those marked with a star are genuinely expensive; this reduces the clientele to a few wealthy Hungarians in a sea of diplomats, business people, and tourists. It's always advisable to reserve in advance to ensure getting a table.

Alabárdos - I. Országház u. 2, tel. 156-0851
Bagolyvár - XIV. Állatkerti út 2, tel. 321-3550
Belcanto - VI. Dalszinház u. 8, tel. 269-3101*
Chicago - VI. Blaha Lujza tér, tel. 269-6753
Cyrano - V. Kristóf tér 7-8, tel. 266-3096*
Fausto's - VII. Dohány u. 5, tel. 322-7806
Fatál - V. Váci u. 67, tel. 266-2607
Gundel - XIV. Állatkerti u. 2, tel. 322-1002*
Halászbástya étterem - I. Hess Andrés tér 1-3, tel. 202-0580
Kacsa - II. Fő u. 75, tel. 201-9992
Légrádi Antique Restaurant - V. Bárczy I. u. 3-5, tel. 118-6804*
Lugas - II. Szilágyi E. fasor 77, tel. 212-2278*
Mágnáskert - II. Csatárka u. 58, tel. 168-6085*
Múzeum - VIII. Múzeum krt. 12, tel. 267-0375
Náncsi Néni - II. Ördög árok u. 80, tel. 176-5809
Robinson Étterem - XIV. Városligeti tó, tel. 342-0955*
Sipos - III. Fő tér 6, tel. 188-8745

KOSHER

Carmel Pince - VII. Kazinczi u. 31, tel. 122-1834

VEGETARIAN

Vegetárium - V. Cukor u. 3, tel. 138-3710

COFFEE HOUSES

Korona - I. Dísz tér 16
Litea - I. Fortuna udvar
Gerbeaud - V. Vörösmarty tér 7
Művész - VI Andrássy út. 29
New York - VII. Erzsébet körút 9-11
Café Remiz - II. Budakeszi út 5
Talk Talk Café - V. Magyar u. 12-14
Café Incognito - VI. Liszt F. tér. 3